CROSSING
THE LINE
A MEMOIR OF RACE, RELIGION, AND CHANGE

CROSSING
THE LINE
A MEMOIR OF RACE, RELIGION, AND CHANGE

By Richard Abercrombie
With JoAnn Borovicka

BELLWOOD
PRESS

WILMETTE, ILLINOIS

Bellwood Press
401 Greenleaf Avenue, Wilmette, Illinois 60091

22   21   20   5   4   3

Library of Congress Cataloging-in-Publication Data

Names: Abercrombie, Richard, author. | Borovicka, JoAnn, author.
Title: Crossing the line : a memoir of race, religion, and change / by
  Richard Abercrombie with JoAnn Borovicka.
Description: Wilmette, Illinois : Bellwood Press, 2019. | Includes
  bibliographical references. | Audience: Ages 12-15 | Audience: Grades
  7-9
Identifiers: LCCN 2019040904 (print) | LCCN 2019040905 (ebook) | ISBN
  9781618511522 (paperback) | ISBN 9781618511546 (ebook)
Subjects: LCSH: Abercrombie, Richard--Juvenile literature. | Bahais--South
  Carolina--Greenville--Biography--Juvenile literature. | Bahai converts
  from Christianity--South Carolina--Greenville--Juvenile literature.
Classification: LCC BP395.A28 A3 2019 (print) | LCC BP395.A28 (ebook) |
  DDC 297.9/3092 [B]--dc23
LC record available at https://lccn.loc.gov/2019040904
LC ebook record available at https://lccn.loc.gov/2019040905

Cover design by Carlos Esparza
Book design by Patrick Falso

I dedicate this book to Mr. Kiser Barnes, who initiated this project by asking me to tell my story, to my son James Richard (Jamie) Abercrombie, Jr., who would not let me forget Kiser's request, and to JoAnn Borovicka, who insisted on writing my story down.

Richard Abercrombie

Contents

Acknowledgments

It is our great pleasure to thank the following friends and family members for their generous assistance with this manuscript. Whether it was sharing your memories in interviews, reading and responding to the manuscript at its various stages, or providing photographs, your help is deeply appreciated: Michael J. Borovicka; Andrea Lavelle Abercrombie; Anita Elaine Abercrombie; Beverly Elaine Abercrombie; Charles Clinton Abercrombie, Jr.; Della Elizabeth Abercrombie; James Richard (Jamie) Abercrombie, Jr.; John Melvin Abercrombie; Phillip London Abercrombie; Sara Cannon Abercrombie; Rodney Vanoy Acker; Jeanne Aguirre; Michael (Big Mike) Aguirre; Joy Suzanne Faily Benson; Kenneth E. Bowers; Victoria Chance; Laurie (CJ) Cohen; Bernadette Cooper; Farzaneh Guillebeaux; Reid Henderson; Elise Hind; Catherine Frances Hosack; Fereydoun Jalali; Bernard Johnson; Frank Jordan; Mary Arlene Kuchakpour; Madelaine Lamb; Mickey Lamb; Virginia Kintz; John (Bo Jack) Mangum; Maryann Maxson; Jack McCants; Damon McGhee; Ernestine Mehtzum; Monika Scott Rogers; Braylon Scott; Ronald Alandrus Smith, Sr.; William (Smitty) Smith; Richard Thomas; Ashley Walker; Carolyn Wells; Kurt Wells; Frances Worthington; and Devon Woung.

We would also like to express our sincere appreciation to Christopher Martin, Bahhaj Taherzadeh, and Nat Yogachandra for their invaluable guidance and support of this project throughout the editing and publication process.

Richard Abercrombie and JoAnn Borovicka

- 1 -

Missing Pieces

Mrs. Broadneck, my biology teacher, was coming at me fast, nostrils flared. It was because of something I'd said. I knew I couldn't get past her to the door, so I went for the open window. I figured it was about a 12-foot drop to the ground, not too bad. I jumped and rolled—didn't break anything. Then I avoided school for the rest of the day. Business as usual.

It was 1960 in Greenville, South Carolina. I was a fourteen-year-old black teenager throwing myself around in a world that didn't make sense to me. I didn't know that in twelve months' time I'd make a different kind of jump, one that would save my life. But before I get into that, let me tell you some more about myself.

My name is James Richard Abercrombie. I go by my middle name, Richard, but most people call me Rick or Ricky. I was the fifth of eight children—six boys and two girls—and we were all encouraged to attend church on Sunday. By "encouraged" I mean that my parents, Charles and Lillie Abercrombie, made it a rule for their children that if you didn't go to church on Sunday, then you weren't allowed to go anywhere or do anything for the rest of that day. But if you did go to church, then you could pretty much do whatever you wanted that afternoon and evening. So I went to church.

Somewhere in the process of this religious coercion, I came to enjoy church and Sunday school, and I embraced Jesus Christ as my Lord and Savior. We had a color glossy picture of Jesus—the Scandinavian-looking Jesus image that has been made so popular over the years. The picture was framed, but not behind glass. When I was about nine years old, on some occasion in which I was filled with gratitude, I felt compelled to kiss that picture. Shortly afterward, on considering my own unworthiness compared to the high station of Jesus, I took a wet towel and reverently wiped the picture where I had kissed it. That particular show of reverence didn't end well for the picture, which was pretty much ruined by that wiping, but my love for Jesus was sincere.

As I grew older, however, I began to question what I had been told about God and religion. It was like pieces of the puzzle were missing. Whenever I looked up into the night sky or watched a sunrise, I felt that there had to be a Creator, but I also thought that I wasn't being told the truth about that Creator. For instance, I wondered how God could—in all of His divine mercy—be OK with people being tortured in hell for an eternity because of some bad decision they made while on Earth. At times, I wondered if the whole God idea was like Santa Claus—something adults told their kids to get them to behave and that somehow the adults just never confessed that the whole thing was all make-believe. There was also the problem of religious teachings I'd heard on the nature of the universe.

When I was growing up, my friends and I were all about space travel. Our interest was fueled by daily news of the space race between the United States and the Soviet Union. Often, when I was walking outside, especially at night, I'd gaze up at the sky. I felt the endlessness of the universe, and I would imagine the fabulous worlds that might be discovered in the cosmos. When I shared my ideas about the infinite universe with Reverend Ferguson (who was working as a substitute teacher for my science class) he disagreed. He told me that, according to the Bible, the universe had an end. I asked him, "But if a spaceship could travel a million miles an hour for a trillion years, it still wouldn't come to the end of the universe, would it?" He said with complete confidence that, according to the Bible, it would. I asked, "What would that end look like?" He said, "There'd be a wall." I asked, "What would be on the other side of that wall?" He couldn't tell me. His insistence that we lived in a closed and limited universe didn't ring true to me, so I had no use for Reverend Ferguson after that.

There were other religious teachings that didn't make sense to me, such as that in all of humanity's long history, Jesus was the only divine Being Who had ever walked the planet. Why, I wondered, would God have abandoned the human race before and after the appearance of Jesus of Nazareth? I was perplexed by the teaching that the only people going to heaven were certain Christians. What about all the other good people in the world? The millions of Buddhists, Muslims, Jews, and everybody else? How about the people who had never even heard about Jesus? And I was disturbed with the apparent rule that black and white people had to attend separate churches. And schools. And restaurants. Where was that in the Gospel?

Why Won't He Fix It?

I was born during the time of government-enforced racial segregation (often referred to as Jim Crow laws), but I didn't notice segregation that much when I was a little child. My world was small, and I was surrounded by a large and loving family. I was also embraced by our neighborhood, Nichol-town, which was an area that measured about ten-by-ten blocks in the city of Greenville. My family knew all of our immediate neighbors and, for the most part, their yards were my yard. If I did something mischievous a half block down the road, my mother would know about it before I got home because there were always neighborly eyes watching out for me. But once I got old enough to venture out of Nicholtown on my own, at around ten or eleven years old, the restrictions and dangers of segregation came into focus, and I felt its hostility.

The Abercrombie children were taught the basic facts of survival for black kids in the 1940s, 50s, and 60s. My mother, who never said an unkind word about anyone, voiced it in her gentle manner. She said, "You've got to feed white people with a long-handled spoon. Be kind, and give them what they need, but don't get too close." This instruction, lovingly offered for the purpose of protecting our lives, was based on years of experience in the Deep South.

There were lots of dos, don'ts, and facts of segregation. Some I was taught, and some I just knew. I knew that all the kids I went to school with were black. I knew that all my teachers were black. Anytime I rode on a bus with white people, I knew I had to sit in the back. I knew that my big brothers and I could walk up Ackley Road to the stop sign safely enough, but I also knew that past the stop sign—the Eastover white area with the ice cream store—was hostile territory. The line of segregation was invisible, but we knew it was there. If we walked past the stop sign, white kids would likely call us ugly names, and we knew we had to leave or we'd get hurt. I knew that my friends and I could walk through Cleveland Park at the bridge but that we were not allowed to stop to play there, even though the park was right next to Nicholtown. That was tragic. Once my little brother Phillip asked my mother, "Momma, does God love everybody?" She said, "Yes, Phillip, He does." Then Phillip asked, "Then why won't He fix it so I can play baseball in Cleveland Park?"

I got my first job outside of Nicholtown shortly after I turned thirteen. I shined shoes every weekday after school at the Airport Barber Shoppe on Pleasantburg Drive. The Barber Shoppe was a white establishment, but shining shoes was a colored person's job, so I got hired. Often my employer would send me over to the café across the street to get coffee and sandwiches for the barbers and the customers. The café was a white business, too. The first time I went on this errand, I placed the order and then sat down on a café chair to wait for the food. The white staff immediately told me that I could not sit down. I had to stand and wait until the order was finished. They all looked at me like I should have known better. So I stood up and waited, as I did with each order thereafter. While everybody acted like this double standard was normal, that I should stand and wait while a white take-out customer could sit and wait, this rule and others like it made no sense to me.

One day I got to the Barber Shoppe late, so my employer fired me. Of course, I was mad about that. As I was leaving, I stopped and took a long look at the café across the street. I couldn't help it. I strolled across Pleasantburg Drive, entered the café, and gave the waiter a big order. Coffees, sodas, doughnuts, sandwiches. They were used to me getting several things for the Barber Shoppe clientele, but this order was especially big. Then I sat down in a café chair. My plan was simple—as soon as they told me that I wasn't allowed to sit down, I would dramatically jump to my feet and shout, "Then cancel the order!" I'd leave in a huff, and that would show them. But they didn't tell me to get up. Nobody paid any attention to me. They were all busy getting my big order together—the order that I didn't have money to pay for. After a few minutes, I told them that there was something I had to do, and I zipped out of the café and disappeared. I don't know who ate all those sandwiches.

In my attempts to find a job other than shining shoes, I learned to not even approach white businesses. Typically, they'd say, "We don't hire coloreds," or "Negroes," or the "n" word. It wasn't logical. Black people supported these businesses, yet these same businesses wouldn't hire blacks. My big brother Charles could buy a pricey suit at a men's clothing store, but that store wouldn't hire him to wait on the customers. These rules of segregation created a heaviness to life. I felt pressed to show respect to authorities, even though the rules these authorities followed made no sense to me. And the older I got, the heavier these burdens became.

In addition to the tensions between the whites and the blacks, as an Abercrombie, I had to contend with another dimension of prejudice. While my family had some African features, we also had relatively light skin and light-colored hair, which created more complications. I had platinum blonde hair when I was born. People called me "Cotton Head." As I got a little older, my hair changed to light brown. My sister Della could pass as a white person pretty much any time she wanted to. Della's friends often asked her to go to the all-white theater to see what was playing or to go to certain evening talks at the white schools and report back about what went on there. She could always get in. But at that time, it was the law that if you had at least one-sixteenth Negro blood in your ancestry, then you were legally a Negro, and all the segregation laws applied to you. It was called the "one drop" rule. Thus, we were "Negroes," but we looked "different."

Where I Came From

I know a few things about the complicated history of my family's coloring.

My Father's Ancestry

My father's grandfather, John Marion Abercrombie (1839–1914), was Scottish. He was born in Scotland, but when he was young, his father and mother brought him and his brothers to the United States, and they settled in South Carolina (in Mauldin, Simpsonville, and Fountain Inn, neighboring towns to Greenville). The Abercrombies owned many acres of land that they farmed, and in the early years they owned slaves. The slaves of the Abercrombies went by the last name of "Crumbie."

Some time after the Civil War and the freeing of the slaves, John Marion married Elizabeth (1852–1909), an African woman who had been born into slavery but then freed. Elizabeth was just as black as John Marion was white. All indications are that this was a loving relationship. Of course, they couldn't get married in South Carolina, so they traveled up north, got married, then came back. For the rest of their lives, Elizabeth and John Marion worked and lived on their farm, which was located between Greenville and Mauldin.

Over the next many years, Elizabeth and John Marion had thirteen children—ten boys and three girls. As you might imagine, their children's skin color ranged from light to dark, and the children had a mix of European and African features. In addition to raising their own children, John Marion and Elizabeth also raised Elizabeth's nieces and nephews, who were the children of Elizabeth's sister who had died in childbirth with her fourth pregnancy.

When John Marion married Elizabeth, his family abandoned him for marrying a black woman. They wouldn't have anything to do with him, and they never met any of the children—that is, until the day of John Marion's funeral. That's right. His brothers showed up outside of the family's church, Laurel Creek Methodist, right before the funeral service.

You have to understand that in the early 1900s, it was against the law in many places for Negroes to be buried in cemeteries designated for white people, and it was unheard of for a white person to be buried in a Negro cemetery. And sure enough, although John Marion's brothers had not seen him for over forty years, they came to get his body so that, as was their notion, John Marion wouldn't go to hell with all those blacks in the Negro cemetery. The first person the brothers met outside the church was John Marion's daughter,

Mary, who by that time was a grown woman. They told Mary, "We've come to take John Marion back home to be buried."

Mary was driving a buckboard at the time. A buckboard is a horse-drawn carriage with a long flatbed made for hauling things on a farm. On this particular occasion, I believe it had been used to transport John Marion's casket to the church.

Word had it that Mary was handy with a gun. She pulled her rifle out from under the seat of the buckboard and told John Marion's brothers, "You didn't have anything to do with him when he was livin', you're not gonna have anything to do with him now that he's dead." Then she said, "You can come in for the service, but then you best turn 'round and go back home." I don't know whether or not his brothers stayed for the funeral service, but they definitely didn't leave with John Marion's body. He's buried in our family plot at the Laurel Creek Methodist Church Cemetery.

John Marion and Elizabeth's son, John Willie Abercrombie (1888–1955), was destined to become my father's father. John Willie was his parents' favorite, and they pampered him in every way. In third grade, his teacher punished him for acting out in class. In response, his parents stopped sending him to school! Nevertheless, John Willie was smart and mechanically inclined. When he grew up, he married Elizabeth Morton (1890–1960). The story of Elizabeth's mother shows how dangerous those times were for black people.

Elizabeth Morton's mother, Maude Morton (born circa 1870, date of death unknown) was a black woman who never married, but she had two children by Will Jenkins, a white man who was the overseer on the farm where she worked. Jenkins was a widower who kept coming around and making sexual advances toward Maude's older sister (whose name I don't know). But when Maude's older sister refused Jenkins' advances, he killed her. There were no legal consequences. After killing her sister, Jenkins targeted Maude, who had no protection from him. Two children came of this situation: Mettie and Elizabeth Morton. These girls never knew their father.

Elizabeth Morton married John Willie Abercrombie, and they had eleven children—nine boys and two girls. One of their boys would become my father, Charles Clinton Abercrombie (1917–1999). Growing up, I knew Great Granny Maude Morton, Granny Elizabeth Morton, and Aunt Mettie Morton well. I remember all three of them as very kind and gentle.

In consequence of all of the above, my father's ancestry was mixed: African (countries unknown), Scottish, and additional white (countries unknown).

My Mother's Ancestry

My mother, Lillie Strange Abercrombie, had a mixed heritage, too. Her great grandfather, Neuton Henry Luster (born 1837, date of death unknown) was from Mali, a country in West Africa. When he was a boy, he and his parents were kidnapped from Mali and sold into slavery in South Carolina. Neuton and his father ended up on neighboring plantations, so they saw each other occasionally. But Neuton never knew what happened to his mother. He heard her being auctioned off on the block, and that was the last he heard of her. Despite their attempts to locate her, he and his father never could find out who bought her or where she ended up.

Neuton grew to be a man of high capacity. His work on the plantation was valued by the owners, plus he had strong and unconventional negotiating skills. He was able to get materials, supplies, and privileges for himself and his fellow slaves that otherwise would not have been forthcoming. Most blacks were afraid of whites, both during slavery and after reconstruction, but not Neuton. Because of his resourcefulness and fearlessness, his family referred to him as "the Pirate."

After the Civil War had ended and enslaved people had gained their freedom, Neuton met Martha (born 1850), a white woman, and they fell in love. Because of the laws of the time, Martha knew that there was no way she could marry Neuton and expect both of them to live unless she passed for black, which meant that she would have to change her legal records and social identity to "Negro." And that's what Martha wanted. She appealed to her father for permission to pass for black and to marry Neuton. Her father gave his permission and gave her away at the wedding ceremony. Unfortunately, on the way home from the wedding, Martha's father got thrown off his horse and died. Some say that the grief of marrying his daughter off to a black man made him commit suicide, that he had somehow made his horse throw him. People said, "He gave Martha what she wanted, then he killed himself." However, that particular interpretation of his death does not sound right to me. Getting thrown from a horse seems like an unlikely way for someone to attempt suicide. I believe his death was accidental.

At any rate, Martha and Neuton married for love (she is listed in the census records as "Negro"), and they had three children—John, Jake, and Sally. Sally was destined to become my mother's grandmother. Sally married Dave Sebrig and had two children, Corry and Jack. I'm not sure what happened there, but the marriage ended. After a while, Sally got married again—this time to Joseph Fowler, a man who claimed to be African, white, and Blackfoot Indian. Sally and her two children took the name "Fowler," and then Joseph and Sally had four children of their own—Della Mae, Collum, George, and Marie. Della Mae (1905–2006) would become my mother's mother.

When she was young—I think thirteen—Della Mae got married to Garfield Strange, a man of African and Cherokee Indian heritage. We're not quite sure of the circumstances of her marriage, but it may not have been entirely voluntary. Della Mae and Garfield had two children: Lillie (1921–2016) who was to become my mother; and Martha. Della Mae and Garfield's marriage ended in divorce after about seven years, but I'll tell you about that later.

Growing up, my mother was close to her grandparents (Sally and Joseph Fowler) and her great-grandparents (Martha and Neuton Luster). One of her favorite stories was how Neuton, who she always referred to as "Grandpappy Neut the Pirate," was fiercely proud of his heritage and quick to tell people, "I'm not an ordinary nigger. I'm Malian."

Generations later, my children Jamie, Andrea, and Anita and a few of their close cousins—impatient with how they were constantly pressed to answer the question "What race are you?"—would invent a word to describe our family's distinctive ancestry. They came up with the term Scoblawhidian. That's short for Scottish, black, white, and Indian.

Because of our relatively light skin and hair color, both white and black people sometimes treated us better than dark-skinned blacks. But there were also times when we were ostracized by blacks because of our European features. We were an oddity on both sides, which made things that much more complicated. I felt as if I was living in three different worlds: my family circle where differences in color were seen as natural; a black circle where I was too light, and a white circle where I was too dark. The complicated color rules in the black and white circles were a constant source of irritation to me.

The Coat Incident

My aggravation with illogical social rules, combined with the doubts I felt about church teachings, became more and more unbearable until I reached a breaking point. This happened on an otherwise normal Sunday morning shortly after I turned thirteen. I think of the occasion as "the coat incident."

Our church, Tabernacle Baptist (the second largest black Baptist church in Greenville), had a dress code stating that all the boys and men had to wear coats, such as a sports jacket or suit coat, while attending church services. I had just left Sunday school, where coats were not required, and I realized that I had left my suit coat in our locked car. My father, who had the keys to our car, was in a deacons' meeting and couldn't be disturbed. Being without a suit coat, I was not allowed inside the sanctuary for the church service. I had to wait outside by myself until the service was over. That was a long hour. The whole time, I thought about how stupid the rule about mandatory coats in church was. Although it may now seem like a small thing, I recall this incident as the point where I snapped—the moment when the number of illogical things I was expected to accept about religion, church, race, the world and my place in it, suddenly became unbearable. I felt let down by all the authorities in my life. So I became an emotional dropout. I segregated myself from caring. In the weeks that followed, I refused to go to church, became disengaged in school, disobedient to my parents, and delinquent in my activities. I was thirteen years old and in the eighth grade. The world did not make sense. Why should I? I threw myself into an attitude of just not caring.

I distanced myself from all the people who had previously been my safe havens—my family, friends, teachers, everybody. This emotional separation hurt, and I felt lonely all the time. To dull the pain, I began drinking alcohol—mostly wine because it was cheap, but sometimes whiskey or beer. My parents did not drink any alcoholic beverages, so I did not get the alcohol from the house. I bought it myself. Of course, it was illegal for a thirteen-year-old to buy alcoholic drinks, but nobody enforced that law. I could get whatever I wanted whenever I wanted it—which I did quite often, even though I actually didn't enjoy drinking. It was not a social activity for me. Most of the time I drank alone.

Whenever I went out for the evening, I'd drink beforehand. If I went to a movie, I'd take a bottle with me. I even drank before I went to school. I got used to facing the world in an intoxicated state. I was often tardy or truant, my grades declined, and my attitude worsened. I had pretty much enjoyed school up to that point, and had done fine in my classes. My family was well-known at school. My father had served as president of the Parent Teacher Association, and my older siblings had reputations as good students. My family was also well-respected at Tabernacle Baptist. My father was a deacon and a member of the board of trustees, and often the preacher would come to our house for dinner. So when I started showing up late to school, missing school altogether, failing classes, refusing to go to church, and acting disrespectfully to just about everybody, people didn't know what to make of me.

When I was a kid, most schools and parents disciplined their children by some sort of physical punishment. Usually parents would give their kids a few swats with a paddle, belt, or a switch. Likewise, my mom and dad occasionally used corporal punishment to keep us in line.

Sometime after the coat incident, I got paddled by my father. For what exactly, I don't remember. It could have been any number of things. So, I got a few swats. But when my father was through, I looked him in the eye (I had to look up) and told him that was the last paddling I was going to take from him. And I absolutely meant it. At the age of thirteen, I thought that I didn't have to abide by my parents' rules, and I was ready to leave home to prove it. In short, I thought I was "grown."

A couple of years earlier, I had heard my father talking to my older brother Charles who was getting restless to leave home because he thought he was grown. My father sat him down and said, "Son, let me tell you about grown.

You're *grown* when you can come in and tell me that you're leaving, and I go upstairs and help you pack your clothes, and you got a place to live, and I help you settle there. Don't think you're grown if you go off for three days and then want to come back here to eat. You're grown when you come back home when you're invited. Now, Son, you can leave home anytime you want, but you need to leave in good standing because you're gonna need my permission to come back."

I knew the rules about "grown." Yet in my befuddled way of looking at things, I was ready to throw myself out the door and take my chances in an absolutely hostile world well outside of any kind of safety net. And, as a first giant step in that direction, I had just challenged my dad by telling him that I was not going to take any more of his paddlings.

Now my daddy was a big man, well over six feet tall. He had a booming voice and piercing blue eyes. His stern presence spoke of authority. In any setting, it was evident that my father was a force to be reckoned with. Frankly, he could have picked me up by the ankles and cleaned the floor with me any time he wanted. But when I challenged him like that, he looked deeply into my eyes but did not say a word. And after that night, he never disciplined me with a paddling again. He knew that I was crazy enough to leave home, and he did not force a confrontation that he knew would have put me out of the house and in the midst of the worst of dangers. I found out later that my parents decided that the best way to handle my rebelliousness was to encourage whatever I did that was good, to be patient with my acting out, and to pray for me.

- 2 -

"That Can't Be My Son"

Over the next few years, I continued drinking on the sly and barely stayed in school. But even with all of my bad behavior, I was not entirely irresponsible. I earned a good bit of money doing part-time jobs that I created myself. I contracted to provide janitorial services for three businesses that occupied the upstairs space of the U.S.O.* building for black servicemen on McBee Avenue: Dr. Gibson's Dental Practice, the F. C. Pickens Insurance Company, and Dr. Kirkland's Medical Practice. All three were black establishments. I'd clean these offices once a week on weekday evenings. I also had my own business doing yard work and mowing lawns on the weekends, which was extremely lucrative. In fact, by the age of fourteen, I made more money on a weekend than a common laborer made all week because I charged by the job and I was fast. I made about $5.00 an hour instead of the typical $1.25. Five dollars was a lot of money back then—the equivalent of about $40.00 by today's (2019) standards. I was interested in making money, and I was good at it. But I was careless with my money. I'd spend it on alcohol and often lose it by gambling with cards or dice.

One summer night when I was fourteen, I bought a bottle of wine and went to see a movie. There were three theaters in Greenville that black people could attend. The Harlem Theater on South Hudson Street and the Liberty

---

* U.S.O. stands for "United Service Organization," a community effort to support soldiers and their families.

Theater on Spring Street were both specifically for colored people. Then there was the Center Theater on Main Street, which had seating for both coloreds and whites. The white entrance was in the front of the building on North Main Street. But to get to the colored entrance, you had to walk down to Brown Street, find the dark dead-end alley that led to the back of the theater building, then go in the back door and up a narrow stairway to the "colored section" balcony. That night I went to the Center Theater and drank my bottle of wine up in the balcony. When the movie was over, I knew I was too intoxicated to walk home, so I decided to catch a taxi. I was making my way as best I could to the Taxi Cab Center on the corner of Spring and Washington Streets when I saw a car coming down the road with a light on top. I thought it was a taxi cab, so I waved it down. But it wasn't a taxi. It was a police car. The two policemen quickly ascertained my condition and arrested me for public drunkenness.

Of course I did not want my parents to find out that I'd been arrested, and I thought that I could contain the damage of the situation by not identifying myself. So I refused to tell the police my name. They put me in jail anyway.

At some point, one of the policemen recognized me as an Abercrombie. (As I mentioned, the Abercrombies looked different.) Going on this clue to my identity, the police called one of Dad's brothers, Uncle Henry, and told him that they might have one of his boys at the jail. Uncle Henry told the police that they couldn't have one of his sons because all his boys were at home. Then the police described my age and appearance, and Uncle Henry determined that it was me, Ricky Abercrombie, Charles' son. The police called my house.

My mother answered the phone. The policeman said, "We've got your son Ricky down here at the police station. He's been arrested for public drunkenness." My mother said, "No, that can't be my son. My son's name is James Richard." The fact is, nobody ever called me "James Richard," but because my mother did not want to believe that I'd been arrested, she argued that it wasn't me. But my father believed it was me. He told the police he'd be down to the station to pick me up. But when he got there, the police wouldn't let me go. They said I was too drunk to be released. My dad told the police that he was my father, he could deal with me being drunk, and that I didn't need to be spending the night in jail. The police released me to him, at which time literally Dad picked me up, threw me into the back of his pickup truck, drove home, and sent me to bed.

The next morning, Dad woke me up early and told me to get ready to go with him to work. I had lawns that I needed to mow, so I told him that I couldn't go with him—I had other work to do. But he said, "No, you're coming with me." Then he took me on probably one of the most strenuous jobs I've ever done in my life—building the spillway at the bottom of what was going to be a man-made lake. My job was to carry mortar and bricks down a steep hill in a wheelbarrow. But that wasn't the hard part. The hard part was pushing the wheelbarrow back up the hill.

In addition, I got a long talking-to from both of my parents about the dangers of alcohol. As for my arrest, the court ordered that I pay a $15.00 fine for my offense (about $120.00 by today's standards). But Judge Hicks, who handled the case, didn't let me pay it off all at one time. He ordered me to pay $3.00 a week for five weeks in person at the courthouse.

The inconvenience of making this weekly trip to the courthouse was part of my punishment. It was bothersome, but neither the embarrassment, the wheelbarrow torment, my parents' displeasure, nor the court fine stopped me from drinking. My rebelliousness continued, and I barely managed to stay in school—it just wasn't important to me. I continued to cultivate a reputation for truancy, bad grades, failure, rowdiness, and overall disrespect. Every once in a while, I'd get suspended from school. But none of that concerned me.

Recreational Activities

Other than the gambling, my social activities were mostly typical of any teenager at the time; it's just that with whatever I was doing, I was intoxicated to some degree. Sometimes I went to dances at the canteens on weekend nights. A canteen was a place that sold snacks, played music, and had a dance floor. It could be set up at a school gym, church hall, or recreation center. Generally, there was a small cover charge to get in. There was a canteen for blacks at the Whitehouse Community Center which was part of the Green

Forest Park recreation complex for blacks near my home. The Whitehouse was exactly as it sounds—a big, old, two-story white house converted to a public facility. There was a swimming pool for blacks behind the Whitehouse, and a skating rink across the street. There were also canteens for black teenagers at Mayberry Park, as well as the Phyllis Wheatley Center on Broad Street in downtown Greenville. I frequented all of those places.

One of the recreational activities of some white teenagers at that time consisted of racing through black neighborhoods. This harassment would happen in Nicholtown pretty much on a weekly basis. A carload of white kids or adults would speed down our streets shouting out obscenities and racial slurs directed to any individual or group of blacks gathered on a corner, a front porch, a playground, wherever. Sometimes there would be shouting along with a firebomb thrown at a house. The whites knew, correctly enough, that there would be no legal repercussion for their behavior, even if the police were called. There was little police response to calls from black neighborhoods. If you did call, the police might not show up until the next day, even if somebody had died. And because the whites were speeding through the neighborhood, there would usually be no time for retaliation. Only sometimes were we successful in making our objections known, like the time my friends turned a dead-end road at the Whitehouse Community Center into a trap.

The road that led to the Whitehouse curved around the back of the building and stopped abruptly in a dead end at the public pool. On this particular evening, there were about a dozen black friends gathered in the parking lot of the skating rink across the street from the Whitehouse when a carload of white teenagers sped by shouting insults. Apparently unaware that the road they were on was about to come to an end, the white teenagers sped around to the back of the Whitehouse. The black teenagers watched in disbelief and amusement because they knew that there was no way for that car to get out except for it to come back the same way it drove in.

Now the teenagers in the skating rink parking lot had some choices. They could have done nothing at all. Or, those with vehicles could have jumped in their cars, blockaded the road, and escalated the situation. Or they all could have picked up rocks and waited for the car to come back by. I'm told there was no conversation. Like birds in a tree that suddenly decide to fly off all at once, those in the parking lot scattered to find rocks—good throwing rocks. After about one quiet minute, the car came screaming back around the curve to make its escape. The rocks flew, and the white kids drove off with a considerably dented car.

The drive-throughs that whites did in black neighborhoods was not something that blacks did in white neighborhoods. To return the harassment would have been suicide. The white neighborhoods actually had police protection. In fact, it was dangerous for a black person to even peaceably walk or drive through a white neighborhood after work hours. Any black presence in a white neighborhood that was not associated with being a maid, a cook, a yard worker, or some other kind of hired labor was reason for that person to be picked up by the police, or worse.

Close Calls

On top of the dangers that came from the white community, there were opportunities to get into trouble just for being a teenager. Like anywhere, dancing with somebody else's girlfriend could be risky. Even venturing outside of your own neighborhood could be problematic. If you lived in Nicholtown, you stayed in Nicholtown, and you definitely didn't date a girl from, say, the Haynie Street or Greenline neighborhoods that were a mile or so away. You just didn't cross that line. It was another kind of prejudice—tribal. I was attacked once by a group of guys, and the only thing I could figure out was that they didn't like that I was seeing a girl from their neighborhood. They beat me until I passed out. When I woke up, they were gone, and so was the girl. But I still didn't stay in my own neighborhood. If I wanted to go someplace else, I'd just go. I had relatives on Haynie Street where my dad grew up, and I'd go there whenever I wanted, my turf or not.

In short, there were many dangers, either from things that might happen with personality differences, or whatever arguments arise between teenagers, or with hostilities between the blacks and the whites. Because of the possibility of running into trouble, weapons were common. Just about every teenage boy I knew carried a knife."

Guns were hard to come by, especially for blacks, but by the age of fifteen I did own a gun—a .25 caliber semi-automatic pistol that I'd secretly bought on the street and kept hidden in my bedroom closet. And it was only by the grace of God that I didn't destroy my life or anyone else's life with it.

My first close call was my plan to rob a gas station. It happened like this: One night after finishing my work at Dr. Gibson's dental office I walked up to the bus stop on McBee Avenue. The stop was right next to a gas station. While I was standing there waiting for the bus, an elderly black man walked up to the gas station with an empty jug, gave the white attendant a handful of pennies, and said he wanted to buy thirteen cents worth of kerosene. At that time, kerosene sold for nineteen cents a gallon, but the black guy didn't have but thirteen cents. The attendant shouted that he wasn't going to pump thirteen cents worth of kerosene, and he threw the pennies in the elderly man's face. The coins flew everywhere and disappeared in the gravel. The black man turned and started to walk away, but then he came back looking for his thirteen cents. I helped him find his pennies. I also decided right then and there that the white gas station attendant was going to have to pay for what he did.

I figured that the best way to get justice in this situation was for me to rob the attendant and the gas station while he was working there. Then I'd give the money to the elderly gentleman who had tried to buy the kerosene. In my mind, that would make things right. I looked over the gas station and the surrounding area and planned it out. I'd rob the store at night after working at Dr. Gibson's office, leave the scene by way of the train yard at the Valentine Packing Company, and then get to my house through the cover of trees in Cleveland Park. Perfect. I didn't know whether I'd have to shoot the gas station attendant or not. But, however it turned out, I figured that justice would be served and I'd make a clean getaway.

When I went to work at Dr. Gibson's office later in the week, I took my pistol with me. I also brought a homemade stocking mask. By a stocking mask, I mean a mask made from a woman's stocking, the kind a burglar might wear. To make a stocking mask, you tie off a stocking about where the knee would be, cut off the toe end, throw it away, and then you put what's left of it on your head. When you pull the stocking down to your chin, your facial features are all distorted so you are unrecognizable, but you can still see. We used to make these kinds of masks for Halloween. But now I was going to rob the gas station attendant with this stocking mask over my face.

That night, after I finished my work at Dr. Gibson's upstairs office, I put the stocking mask on and then pulled my coat hood onto my head. I had my pistol in my coat pocket. But as I was leaving the office and walking down the stairs to get to the door of the building, Dr. Gibson unexpectedly came around the downstairs corner and started walking up the stairs. He looked up and saw me with the mask over my face and said, "Whoa! Whoa! Whoa! What have we got here?"

I pulled the stocking off. It was an awkward moment.

Dr. Gibson told me to come into his office and have a seat. He said, "Ricky, you need to change your plans for the night." Then he called my house and got my older brother Charles. Dr. Gibson said, "Charles, you need to come here and pick up Ricky. He's up to something. I don't know what it is, but it's no good." Charles picked me up, no questions asked. Later that week, I noticed that the gas station attendant was no longer working there. I never did see him again.

It was about a month or so later. I had just bought a bottle of wine, and I was walking down the road with it on my way to somewhere when three black teenagers I knew stopped me and asked me what I had in the bag. I showed them the bottle. Jimmy, the ringleader who had always been a bit of a bully, thought it would be a good idea if the three of them sat on me while they drank the wine. And that's what they did. They thought they'd pulled off a hilarious practical joke. But they had no idea how crazy I was feeling. I was ready to strike out at in anger at anything within my reach—including and especially these three guys who had humiliated me on the street. I decided I was going to have to give them payback, but how to do it? At this point, my pistol seemed like just the tool I needed to get the justice I craved. I didn't have my gun on me at the time, but I decided that, sometime over the next few weeks, I'd shoot them. One at a time. I wouldn't shoot to kill, but I'd use my pistol to make things right. The severity of my plan for vengeance, in comparison with the relative harmlessness of their practical joke, didn't occur to me.

As it happened, about a week after that incident, Jimmy, the first one on my list and the instigator, got stabbed in a fight at the Ghana Motel and Lounge. I figured that would do as his punishment. Shortly after that, the second guy was arrested, found guilty of a crime, and sent to prison. There was only one left for my vengeance, but because he was a friend of my older brothers, I had second thoughts about shooting him. When he was at the house one afternoon a few weeks after the wine incident, I reminded him of what he had done, described my plan for vengeance, and called his attention to what had happened to the other two. Then I told him that if he would just stand still and let me hit him with my fist one time, just one time, I'd forgive him and wouldn't have to shoot him. He thought I was kidding. He laughed and walked away. I was thinking that it was really too bad that I'd have to shoot this guy, but before I could make it happen, he was cut badly in a fight, and I figured that injury would do as his penalty.

It did occur to me, upon reflecting on the fate of these three practical jokers, that bullying and disrespect inevitably brought its own punishment. At any rate, because of circumstances outside of my control, this was the fourth time I had been saved from using my gun in what would have been heinous crimes. But then there was the fifth time when I actually pulled the trigger.

Around dusk one summer evening in 1961, I was with a few friends at the park near my home when a car of white teenagers sped by screaming obscenities and racial insults. Something had to be done. Now it just so happened that on that evening, I had my pistol in my waistband. As the car passed, I pulled out my gun, released the safety, pointed it at the car, and pulled the trigger. Click. No shot rang out. I was aggravated at the time, but I've thanked God hundreds of times since then for that misfire.

I was fifteen years old and about to start my sophomore year at Sterling High School. I was mad at the world, hungry for justice, and intoxicated much of the time. I had a gun, and I was willing to use it. I was on a fast train to jail or an early grave.

The Invitation

Not too long after that misfire, in late August of 1961, I was invited to a birthday party for a classmate, Helen Strawder. The party was being held at the home of the Benson's, a family I'd never met. But what was bizarre was that their address, 5 Overbrook Circle, was in one of the white neighborhoods in Greenville. It was risky to walk into a white neighborhood after work hours, but I felt like I had to go see what this was all about. As I approached Overbrook, I imagined what would happen if a policeman saw me. He'd most likely put me into the back seat of his patrol car and ask things like: "What are you doing here? What party? Who do you know at that address?" I might be taken to jail. I felt apprehensive, but I found the house and knocked on the front door anyway.

The door opened, and I was warmly welcomed by Richard (Dick) and Joy Benson, a white couple. They invited me in through the front door of their big two-story house. The experience was surreal. That moment was the first time I had ever been let inside of a white person's home through the front door. Before that evening, the only time I'd ever been in a white home was when I was allowed into Mrs. Grady's kitchen. Mrs. Grady was a white yard work client of mine, and sometimes she'd let me in through the back door of her house to have lunch in the kitchen with her maid. But the Bensons invited me into their home through their front door. I felt dizzy as I stepped over the threshold.

I walked with Joy and Dick through the foyer to a sparsely furnished living room. Besides the hard-back chairs, its most prominent feature was a big Oriental rug. I was seated with about fifteen other people. They included a few white people I didn't know as well as black friends of Helen's—most of whom I did know. A white man with a strong southern accent, Dr. Bill Tucker, was speaking to the group. I was unimpressed and irritated when I heard him talking about religion. I intentionally closed my ears. I felt that no white man should be trying to tell black people about God. What I knew about white people's religion was that they used the Bible to support treating blacks the way they did. They used the Bible to oppress people. In addition, his strong white southern drawl, which to me represented everything that was unjust in the world, irritated me to my very bones.

My ears were closed, but my eyes were open. I noticed that a certain elderly white lady in the room, Junie Faily, had an amazing glow on her face and radiated happiness. I wondered where that glow came from.

Later, I learned that Junie Faily and her husband, John, were Joy Benson's parents and that they lived with the Benson family—Joy and Dick and their three toddlers. Both the Failys and the Bensons were members of the Bahá'í Faith, a religion I had never heard of before. Junie had met my classmate Helen while attending Sunday service at Helen's church, Springfield Baptist. (Bahá'ís are encouraged to "Consort with the followers of all religions in a spirit of friendliness and fellowship."[1] and one of the ways that Junie accomplished this outward-looking fellowship was by attending various church services in Greenville.) I thought that Junie must be the only white person attending a black church in all of South Carolina. My classmate Helen had become friends with both the Failys and the Bensons, and she sometimes babysat the Benson's children. The two couples had planned to celebrate Helen's birthday immediately after holding a fireside that evening. ("Fireside" is a term Bahá'ís use to refer to meetings that present information and invite discussion about the teachings of the Bahá'í Faith.) And that is how I stumbled into my first Bahá'í meeting.

I signed the Benson's guestbook that evening because everybody else did, and within a week I got an invitation to return to their home for another fireside. The Failys and Bensons seemed to be nice people, but I had no intention of ever seeing them again. Horace Nash, a friend who had also attended Helen's party, told me he suspected that the Bensons and Failys were communists. At that time, many civic authorities, as well as Protestant leaders (including Bob Jones University in Greenville) and grassroots organizations such as the White Citizens' Council, promoted the idea that all efforts at racial integration were communist-inspired.* In addition, it was a common assumption in the black community that if a white person was nice to a black

---

* For more information on the conflation of anti-integration and anti-communism, see Venters, *No Jim Crow Church,* pp. 203–5.

person, there had to be an ulterior motive. Because of our suspicions, Horace and I discarded any notion of responding to the Bensons' invitation.

A couple of weeks later, I was riding on a city bus that went through downtown Greenville. As the bus was going down South Main Street, I noticed a lady with silver hair walking in the same direction that the bus was traveling. Even though I could only see the back of her, I could tell that it was Junie Faily, the white woman at the Benson's fireside/party who had impressed me with her glowing countenance. As the bus began to pass her, I turned to get a good look at her face. I wanted to catch her off-guard, to see the real Junie—what she looked like when not putting on a show. But there she was with that same radiant glow. I continued to wonder where that glow came from.

- 3 -

Listening

The next month, September of 1961, I got another invitation to a Bahá'í fireside—this time at a different location. The day of the event, I asked Horace if he'd gotten the invitation, too. He said that he had. I said, "I'll see you there." We both laughed, knowing neither one of us planned to attend. Later that same day, one of the teachers at school, Mrs. Ruby Jones, asked me to help backstage with the class play. I think she knew I had once enjoyed being in school plays, and I suspect she thought this activity might help pull me back into good behavior. I thought her invitation was odd because a few days earlier I'd been involved in a physical altercation with her husband, Mr. Jones, the Shop and Mechanical Drawing teacher.

It happened like this: While in Mr. Jones' class, I wanted to leave to smoke a cigarette, so I asked to be excused to go to the bathroom. He said, "No." I thought, "Now, how does he know whether or not I need to go to the bathroom?" So I told him I was going anyway. When I turned to leave, he picked up a wooden block and threw it at me, but missed. I picked up the same block and threw it back at him, hitting him hard in the chest. He hadn't tried to dodge it or anything. He looked at me in shock. I ran as fast as I could out of his classroom and spent the rest of the day hanging out at the Huddle Soda Shoppe a few blocks from school. The next day, I went back to Mr. Jones' class and neither one of us said anything about it.

In spite of this incident, or maybe because of it, Mrs. Jones asked me to help backstage with the school play. I agreed and promised to go to the dress rehearsal that night. At some point during the rehearsal, while I was standing backstage alone in the dark, something told me I had to go to the Bahá'í meeting being held that night. The feeling was so compelling that I could not resist it. I told the teacher who was directing the play that I had to leave. She objected, saying, "This is the dress rehearsal, you can't leave now!" I told her I had to leave but that I'd be back. She turned and walked away.

On my way out the door, I realized I had thrown away the invitation with the address of the fireside written on it. However, I did remember the street name—Anderson Road. It was only about one mile from school, an easy walk. When I reached Anderson Road, I had to decide whether to go left or right. Anderson Road is a long street, and I didn't know which way to turn. I felt drawn to the right, so that's the way I went. After walking a couple of blocks, I saw several cars parked in front of a house. I knocked on the door. Mrs. Shumate, a black woman, answered. I told her I was looking for a Bahá'í meeting. She said, "You're in the right place, come on in." This time, God took pity on me. Although the people gathered in the house were black and white, this meeting was in a black household—the home of the Shumates—and I felt more comfortable. And, most importantly, there was a black person—someone I could relate to—speaking to the group.

The presenter was a tall lady by the name of Eulalia Barrow Bobo. She was about the age of my grandmothers, and she was talking about the Bahá'í Faith.* She had a kind of rugged elegance about her. I was impressed with her manner of speaking, her firm but reasoned conviction. Her explanations were clear without being emotional, dramatic, or pushy. She was talking about the Bahá'í principle of independent investigation of truth, that every person—unconstrained by tradition—has the responsibility to seek out spiritual truth. I was, well, flabbergasted. I felt like much of what I had been told to believe about religion in the past had been defended on the grounds that those beliefs *were* traditional. Now here was a religion that called for my

---

* For more information on the life of Eulalia Barrow Bobo, see *Lights of the Spirit*, edited by Gwen Etter-Lewis and Richard Thomas; and Venters, *No Jim Crow Church*, pp. 199, 218–19, 226.

own inquiry and reasoning, that invited me to look beyond tradition. All the chairs were taken, so I took a seat on the floor near Eulalia.

Next, Eulalia talked about the oneness of humanity—that, according to Bahá'í teachings, there is only one race, the human race. And while we see differences of culture, class, and ethnicity, we are all members of the same human family. The Bahá'í Faith, explained Eulalia, teaches that human beings are spiritually and organically one, and calls for the elimination of all prejudices. The idea of the organic oneness of humanity spoke to my heart. She explained that prejudices of all kinds—these false perceptions—blind us to the fact that every person is a spiritual being with unique abilities, a "mine rich in gems of inestimable value."[1] I looked across the room and noticed an elderly white man in a suit. I thought, "I should be seeing this guy as a mine rich in gems of great value." I was also very aware that this was not something I was naturally inclined to do. The white guy looked my way, and we locked eyes for several moments. I sensed he was thinking the same of me. We both smiled.

At this point, I remembered I'd promised to go back to school for the dress rehearsal. I felt an unfamiliar desire to be true to my word to a teacher. I ran to school only to find that the rehearsal was over and that everyone had left. So, breathing hard, I ran back to the Bahá'í fireside.

I've Been Looking

As I entered the Shumates' house for the second time that evening, Eulalia was explaining another Bahá'í principle—that all of the world's great faiths have one divine Source and represent one unfolding religion. I was so excited about what I was hearing that I could not sit down. Eulalia said that this Bahá'í way of understanding the connection between the major religions is called "progressive Revelation," a process whereby God nourishes and guides humanity through a succession of divine Messengers Who release new capacities into the human world and inspire the progress of civilization. Each Messenger, she explained, brought laws and teachings most suited to the problems and capacities of the age in which They appeared. But although Their social laws may differ, the same eternal truths, such as love and justice, could be found in all of Their teachings. I thought, "I knew it! The Golden

Rule. Do unto others as you would have them do unto you. I knew it had to be in every religion!"

Eulalia got out her "progressive Revelation" chart on which was written some of the divine Messengers that had appeared throughout history. She talked through the chart as we passed it around:

Progressive Revelation of the Word of God
Krishna (Hinduism, about 3100 BC)
Abraham (Judaism, about 1800 BC)
Moses (Judaism, about 1200 BC)
Zoroaster (Zoroastrianism, about 600 BC)
Buddha (Buddhism, about 500 BC)
Jesus Christ (Christianity, about 30 AD)
Muhammad (Islam, 610 AD)
Bahá'u'lláh (Bahá'í Faith, 1863 AD)

That moment was the first time I saw or heard the name *Bahá'u'lláh*, Who was the Founder of the Bahá'í Faith. When I held the chart, I focused on His name, trying to take it in. Eulalia said that Bahá'u'lláh was Arabic for "Glory of God." *Bahá* means "Glory," *'u'* means "of," and *lláh* means "God." I whispered Bahá'u'lláh's name again and again until it rolled off my tongue just the way Eulalia pronounced it: Ba-ha-ul-LAH. I treasure that first moment of what became a lifetime of learning about Bahá'u'lláh's life, mission, sufferings, and teachings.

Pointing to the chart, Eulalia explained that, according to the Bahá'í Faith, all of these Messengers have been part of a divine process whose goal is humanity's spiritual and material salvation. Progressive Revelation, she said, is how divine Providence has nurtured and guided humanity throughout history. Then, quoting Bahá'u'lláh from one of her books, she said that this process could be described as "the changeless Faith of God, eternal in the past, eternal in the future."[2]

My heart was racing. I could feel the truth in those words. I wanted to know more and I had a lot of questions. Right then, Mrs. Shumate invited everyone to get some refreshments. I wasn't hungry, not for food anyway. I managed to corner Eulalia while everybody else was getting snacks. Eulalia acted like she had all the time in the world, and I rolled on with my questions.

I asked, "Does Bahá'u'lláh claim to be the greatest Messenger of God?" I listened carefully to her response, expecting to hear the same claims of one-upmanship and belittling of other religions that I had heard from preachers. But Eulalia said, "No, Bahá'u'lláh states that all of the Messengers of God have the same knowledge and power. They are spiritually One. The differences in Their teachings have to do with the capacities and needs of the people at the time that They appear."

Completely baffled, I said, "Really?" Maybe it was the expression on my face, but Eulalia broke out laughing and said, "Yes, really!"

I continued, "Does Bahá'u'lláh claim to be the last Messenger of God?"

Eulalia said, "No," and she explained that the process of progressive Revelation will go on and on. She added that Bahá'u'lláh did state that the next Messenger would not come before one thousand years have passed. Of course, I wanted to figure out what year that would be. Eulalia suggested that the date to count from would be 1852, the year that Bahá'u'lláh began His mission. I did the calculation, 1852 + 1000 years, and said with astonishment, "You mean that the next Messenger of God will come in or after the year 2852? I thought we'd blow the Earth up long before then!"

We laughed, but my dark expectations were real. Only sixteen years prior, the world was in the middle of World War II. My dad served in the Army during that war. Twenty-five years before that, the United States was fighting in World War I. In fact, my whole World History class was a list of one war after another. I saw the pattern of violence, and I knew that things between the United States and the Soviet Union were tense. But now, in 1961, the stakes were higher than ever. More countries had nuclear weapons. Everybody I knew had bomb shelter plans. Civil defense shelters were located throughout Greenville, with some of them in the basements of schools and churches. I figured we'd use the basement of our house as a bomb shelter since it was mostly underground. A lot of ministers preached that the end of the world was near, and I figured they were right.

The idea that humanity would progress into the year 2852 and beyond was a happy thought! But why so long until the next Messenger? Eulalia replied that she couldn't say, but knowing even some of Bahá'u'lláh's teachings about what humanity was destined to achieve in this era, she figured it was going to take at least a thousand years for the world to get some things right. She said she'd share more about Bahá'í teachings at the next fireside.

By then it was after ten o'clock. Mrs. Shumate thanked all of us for coming and invited everybody to come to the next fireside, which would be at the Benson's house the following evening (Saturday). Before I left the Shumates, the elderly white guy I'd made eye contact with earlier came up to me and introduced himself. His name was Luther Silver. He asked me what I thought of the meeting. I said, "I think it was wonderful." He placed both of his hands firmly on my shoulders, looked into my eyes, and tearfully said, "Son, I have been looking for these people all my life!"

I'm not sure how I got home that night. Maybe somebody gave me a ride. Maybe I walked. Maybe I flew—I know I felt like I could. Everybody at my house had gone to bed by the time I got home. I remember feeling new and alive, and there was this big smile on my face that came from deep inside of me—a place I hadn't heard from in a long time. I wanted to go out and hug the world. I also knew that I had to get up early in the morning and do yard work all day. So I went to bed and fell sound asleep—without my usual alcoholic nightcap.

Left the Station

The next morning, I got up early, went down to the kitchen, and greeted my parents with hugs. I thanked Mom for the breakfast and thanked Dad for the coffee. I ate with gusto, washed my dishes and theirs without being asked, commented on the beauty of the morning, inquired about their plans for the day, and went off to work after giving them more hugs. I noticed the side-glances between them and the raised eyebrows. For the past couple of years, I hadn't had much to say to anybody and certainly was not the herald of happiness. But that morning, my joy overflowed. I sailed through my lawn work, was home in time for dinner, laughed a lot, did my chores, and then headed to the Bensons' fireside.

My heart beat rapidly as I stepped into the Overbrook neighborhood, but I continued just the same. When I got to the Bensons,' I was warmly welcomed again. Eulalia started the meeting by inviting us to say prayers. Then she introduced the topic she had promised, a selection of Bahá'í principles. She explained that these teachings were part of God's current lesson plan and what humanity is *destined* to achieve in this era. She gave everyone a card and asked me to read it aloud:

A Selection of Bahá'í Principles

- Realization of the oneness of humanity
- Knowledge of progressive Revelation
- Elimination of all forms of prejudice (racial, class, national, religious, etc.)
- Realization of the harmony of religion and science
- Adoption of one universal auxiliary language

I finished reading the front of the card and stopped, thinking that was it. I figured it would take a thousand years just to eliminate racial prejudice, let alone accomplish all those other things. But there was more. Eulalia told me to flip the card over and keep reading:

- Equality of women and men in all endeavors
- Compulsory education for all of the children in the world
- Establishment of a world tribunal for the peaceful settlement of disputes between nations
- Justice as the ruling principle in human society
- The establishment of a permanent and universal peace on earth

I can't say that I understood the depth of all of these teachings, but my feeling was that if just some of these things were accomplished, we would have heaven on earth. At the same time, I shook my head and said aloud, "All this is impossible." With complete assurance, Eulalia answered, "Nothing is impossible if it is the will of God."

I learned a lot that evening. One thing that particularly caught my attention was the need for a universal auxiliary language—one language that everyone in the world would learn in addition to their native tongue. Bahá'u'lláh said, "When this is achieved, to whatsoever city a man may journey, it shall be as if he were entering his own home."[3] Eulalia explained that a common language would help eliminate the suspicion people felt for those who didn't speak their language, would make international communication easy, and would be an important step toward world peace.

The need for a common language made sense to me, and it also made the situation in 1961 seem a little crazy. After World War II, most U.S. schools took German out of their foreign language programs. We'd just been in war with Germany. Did that suffering not indicate a need for clearer communication? Why stop talking to Germans? Anyway, I could see how one common language would be a great help in peace efforts. We're all Earthlings. We should be able to talk to each other.

The principle of the equality of women and men rang true to me right away, and I was glad that Bahá'u'lláh espoused it. The Bahá'í view on this topic is that women and men have always been equal in the sight of God, but the male sex has dominated women in the past because of men's more aggressive nature, both physical and mental. But this imbalance is now changing as intuition, love, service, and other spiritual qualities in which women are especially strong are gaining dominance.[4] Eulalia explained that, in this new age, the male and female elements of civilization will work together in greater balance like the two wings of a bird, and gender equity in all human endeavors will help to bring about world peace.

I thought about Mom and Dad. It was clear that they had an equitable relationship. He was almost twice her size and had a forceful personality, but I never once saw him act in an intimidating way toward her. Her voice was heard and valued in every matter. Dad had great respect for Mom, and it showed.

My parents also raised all of us with the strict rule that a boy should never strike a girl. I was not allowed to punch Della (my older sister), no matter what she did. And let me tell you, Della was more than capable of defending herself *and* her brothers in any situation. But it was obvious that this rule of respect for the female sex was not the case in all households. Preachers taught that women should submit to their husbands in all things, and I regularly witnessed men and boys lording this law of male dominance over women and girls. To give just one example:

One day as I was waiting at a bus stop drinking a bottle of soda pop, I saw a disheveled woman come out of a house across the street. A man came out of the same house and started beating her. I couldn't stand it. I repositioned the bottle in my hand to use it as a weapon (at that time, all soft drinks were sold in heavy glass bottles) and started to make my way across the street with the intent of assaulting the man who was beating the woman. But before I got to them, a hand grabbed my shoulder and pulled me back. It was a guy who'd run out of a barber shop to stop me. "Don't you dare interfere with that," he said. "That's how they do." It was general consensus that the business between a man and "his wife" was nobody else's business and that the man legitimately had the upper hand, both literally and figuratively. I backed off with my bottle, but I knew the situation was wrong.

I was happy to learn about Bahá'í teachings on the historical problem of unchecked testosterone, the important role of feminine qualities in establishing world peace, and the expectation of greater gender balance in all things in the future. I recall Eulalia saying, "Gender equity is part of the will of God for this age. The equity train has left the station. People need to wake up and get on the train, or they'll be left behind."

The evening was full of fascinating and hopeful information as well as laughter. Eulalia promised to meet with me early the next day (Sunday) and Dick Benson gave me a ride home. I went to sleep that night even happier than the night before. And still sober.

Rays of One Light

The next day, Sunday, I enjoyed a private all-day fireside with Eulalia at the Bensons' home. Eulalia actually lived in California, but she was visiting Greenville on the invitation of the Bensons. I'd like to mention here that

Eulalia drove all the way from California to South Carolina by herself in her 1957 Chevrolet. For a black woman to drive cross-country into the Deep South in the early 60s—well, it was awfully dangerous. But Eulalia was fearless.

While in Greenville, Eulalia lived at the Bensons' home. As I mentioned before, in my experience, black people didn't walk in through the front door of a white home, let alone live there (except maybe in servants' quarters). So the fact that Eulalia was living with the Bensons *as a part of their family* was amazing to me. However, the Bahá'ís acted like this close association was normal. Their actions demonstrated the central principle of the Bahá'í Faith— the oneness of humanity. "Regard ye not one another as strangers," writes Bahá'u'lláh. "Ye are the fruits of one tree, and the leaves of one branch."[5]

My questions that morning had to do with Bahá'í teachings related to Jesus. I asked, "What does Bahá'u'lláh say about the ascension of Jesus Christ?" My church's claim that Jesus rose bodily up to heaven was, I thought, illogical. Why would acceptance of the great teachings of Jesus Christ require belief in His breaking laws of nature?

Eulalia's response honored the story of the ascension of Christ but also explained it in a way that made sense to me. She said that from a Bahá'í perspective, "heaven" symbolizes the realm of the spirit, and the story of Christ's ascension means that the essence of Jesus Christ—that is, His station as the Word of God—continues eternally in a spiritual manner, "eternal in the past, eternal in the future."[6] I could accept the Bahá'í understanding of the ascension of Christ, and I was glad to hear it.

I asked about the prophecy that when Christ returned He would come with the clouds of heaven.[7] Our church taught to expect this scripture to be fulfilled in a material manner—that the physical body of Jesus would zoom down to Earth on a cloud and that everybody in the world would see Him. Eulalia explained a symbolic meaning of the "cloud" prophecy. "Clouds block the light," she said. "You can't see the sun when it's behind a cloud. And when clouds come to earth, when it's real foggy, you can't hardly see what's in front of you. Think of what might block a person's heart from the appearance of the Word of God—materialism, faulty expectations, misunderstandings—these are clouds of the heart and mind that could keep people from recognizing the Messenger of God for this Day."

She explained that, in every new Revelation, the Messenger of God is always initially denied due to the "clouds" that blind most people to that Messenger's spiritual reality. According to the Bahá'í teachings, the biblical verses about Christ's return with the clouds expressed the circumstances of the next Messenger perfectly—in the symbolic language of scripture.

Eulalia gave several other examples of how the literal interpretation of scripture clouds people's perceptions. I drank in her words like a person dying of thirst. A couple of years before, I had walked away from church, the Bible, and Jesus because I could not accept so many teachings that defied logic— like the idea that Jesus rose bodily into the sky and would someday ride back to Earth on a cloud, at which time only those who believed these and other what I considered irrational teachings would be "saved." It had never occurred to me that there could be another way to understand and honor that scripture. Suddenly I realized that rejecting certain literal interpretations of the Bible wasn't the same as denying Christ Himself. I could embrace Jesus Christ, the biblical scripture, *and* reason! The moment I got this concept, my heart jumped, tears came to my eyes, and I just broke down and cried for joy! I felt like I had come home to my own self. Eulalia put her arm around me and said, "It's OK. I know."

We took a break. Joy served us cookies and tea and sat with us. She and Eulalia asked about my family, school, and pastimes. I shared what I thought I could. I didn't mention that I had been barely staying in school or that my pastimes had included gambling, drinking, and seeking vengeance.

After our tea break, Eulalia explained that the truth of scripture can get muddled because generations of religious leaders impose their interpretations on the teachings of the divine Messenger. Sometimes the religious leaders' motivations are pure and sometimes they are selfish, but either way, the result is man-made doctrines that can lead people astray. Eulalia said that there was a difference between Christianity and what she called "churchianity."

The Bahá'í Faith, she said, wholly embraces the Spirit of Christ and is in complete harmony with Christianity. The Faith did, however, separate itself from church doctrines because it saw many of them as man-made.

I remember my next question as clear as if I asked it today: "Who does Bahá'u'lláh claim to be in relationship to Jesus Christ?" As Eulalia got out her progressive Revelation chart, she said, "Bahá'u'lláh's claim, and what I believe, is that He is the Messenger of God for this Day as Jesus Christ was the Messenger of God in His Day." Then I learned another term, "Manifestation of God."

The Bahá'í writings often refer to the unique spiritual station of the Messenger of God as the "Manifestation" of God because these divine Emissaries perfectly manifest God's will for the age in which They appear. The Bahá'í Faith describes all of the Founders of the world's great religions as Manifestations of God. They have appeared at different times and places when religion needed to be renewed, and They all came from the same Source. Eulalia said that They are "like the rays of one Light." Jesus Christ came as the Manifestation of God almost two thousand years ago. Bahá'u'lláh came as the Manifestation of God for this age. She explained that they are both among a series of Manifestations Who came not to create competing faith systems, but rather to progressively guide humanity and awaken new capacities for the purpose of advancing spiritual and material civilization.

Then it hit me—the expectation of the Return of Christ. I hesitated, but finally got it out: "Is Bahá'u'lláh the Return of Christ?" Eulalia responded, "Is the sunbeam today the return of the sunbeam of yesterday?" She explained that we might say "no" because there are differences of time and circumstance. But in another sense, we might say "yes" because all sunbeams come from the same source and manifest the same attributes of the sun. Similarly, Bahá'u'lláh is not the return of the literal Jesus of Nazareth. There are differences of time and circumstance. But in another sense, Bahá'u'lláh is the Return of the spiritual reality of Jesus, the Christ Spirit, because both Christ and Bahá'u'lláh come from the same Source, possess the same attributes of God, and have the same purpose—to guide mankind to greater expressions of love, justice, and unity.

At the end of the day, I left the Bensons' feeling happier than ever, and after that weekend I continued to go to every Bahá'í gathering I could. It was like I had been starving to death and now here was this banquet set before me. As I feasted, I became a different person overnight. And I mean overnight. My crossing the line from the darkness into the light was faster than my eighth-grade transition into the darkness. I made it to school on time. I did my homework. I felt absolute joy and I wanted to share that joy. I was kind and respectful to everyone, including my teachers. I got rid of the gun and stopped gambling. I had stopped drinking and didn't even miss it.

My overnight change got a lot of attention. Some of my teachers actually came by the house to talk to my mother about my sudden transformation. Schoolmates and teachers asked what was going on with me: "Why the change?" I told them I was studying the Bahá'í Faith. Xanthene Norris, my history teacher, told me, "You're not smart enough to be a Bahá'í." She knew something about the Faith and was aware of the elevated nature of its teachings. In one sense, she was right. Up to that time I'd barely passed my classes and had shown little indication of being smart. But the Bahá'í teachings were not beyond my comprehension. In fact, the Bahá'í teachings made more sense to me than anything else in the world. They helped me make sense out of my life. I felt deeply connected to God's will, and I felt a new love and respect for those around me. The reverence for the divine that I felt as a child was fully alive again. And I didn't have to jump out of any more windows or anything.

- 4 -

Inquisitions and Confirmations

My parents were pleased with the new improved Ricky but baffled by my overnight transformation. It was like a miracle. My brother Charles said I was like a light bulb that had been turned off, then somebody flipped the switch and I was on. "Not a fluorescent light that may flicker a little while before it comes on," he said, "No. Ricky was on the binary system. At first, Ricky was off. Then enter the Bahá'í Faith, and Ricky was on." I was later told that my mother and father mused, "If there's something going on here that can make Ricky change just like that, we might need some of it." They were curious about what it was that jump-started my life for the better. At the same time, Mom and Dad were suspicious of new religious teachings and concerned about my attendance at Bahá'í meetings. They privately discussed what they should do about it.

Their first strategy was to spy on me. Mom and Dad asked my older sister, Della, to go with me to a Bahá'í fireside so that they could get her opinion about what was going on there. I'm sure they felt she was perfect for the job. Della had always been a shrewd judge of character, could quickly size up any situation, and was not afraid of anything.

Della was not a big girl, but when she was a teenager she played football with the boys. One time, when she was running for a touchdown, Robert Lee Simmons, who was quite a bit bigger than Della, tried to tackle her by jumping on her back. Undaunted, she carried Robert and the football over the goal line. Della would run with, over, or through anybody to advance the ball. It got to the point that when Della joined a neighborhood football game, kids would wander off and the game would come to an end. The guys thought she was too rough.

So, Della was chosen to scope out the Bahá'í meetings. She and her husband, Robert (Bobby) Settles, accompanied me to a fireside. Later, I learned Della reported that "All we saw was people loving each other and getting along. It doesn't look communistic or anything." After Della's spy assignment, she and Bobby continued going to firesides for their own enjoyment. My parents progressed to intervention strategy Number 2—inquisitions by my father.

These evening inquiries began in late October 1961. Whenever I got home from a fireside, Dad would be waiting for me, or he'd show up in a minute or two. It didn't matter if he was in the bed sleeping when I tiptoed into the house. He'd appear every time. My brother Charles used to say that my parents could hear a pin drop on cotton, and I believe he was right.

I had shared with my parents the Bahá'í concept of progressive Revelation—that Moses, Jesus, and the Founders of all of the world's great religions appeared as the Word of God in the past, and that now Bahá'u'lláh had appeared as the Word of God for this day. That notion agitated my dad, and he brought out every Bible verse he thought could refute it. His first argument was that only Jesus was the Word of God, and if Jesus had appeared again, everybody would know it because the sun and moon would be darkened and all the stars would fall. I responded from the Bahá'í writings that the sun and moon *were* darkened and the stars *had* fallen. I said, "Dad, think about what those verses mean." I pointed out that the sun and the moon give light and that stars can be used for navigation. So the sun, moon, and stars make perfect symbols of religious leadership which *should* offer people lights of divine guidance as they navigate their lives. "But because religious leadership has gotten all tangled up with manmade doctrines and false teachings, the traditional stars of religious guidance *have* fallen," I said. "That's one of the reasons why it's time for religion to be renewed today." I figured this explanation would make sense to him. Years ago, as a child in church, I had heard my dad challenge something the minister had said that my dad felt was outside the spirit of the Gospel. But Dad clearly wasn't ready to hear biblical interpretations from me.

Another night it was all about names. "How could Bahá'u'lláh be the appearance of the Word of God when His name is not Jesus Christ"? he asked. I pointed out where the Book of Revelation states that the Spirit of Christ would come with a new Name.[1] That was a short conversation. Another time Dad read that upon the coming of Christ, the dead would rise from their graves.[2] "Since that hasn't happened," he challenged, "how could you believe that the Word of God has come again?" I explained the Bahá'í understanding, that with the appearance of the Word of God, many of those who had been spiritually dead would be spiritually awakened. I held up my hands and said, "Dad, the proof is sitting right here in front of you. I was dead in the grave of disbelief and transgression. Now I'm alive. Can't you see that?" He got up, filled his coffee cup, and started on a different topic.

It Wasn't You

After one long debate session, I protested, "Dad, When I was getting into trouble at school and with the law, you never gave me such a hard time as you do now that I am trying to straighten out my life." He answered, "I know that being a teenager is hard and you can get a little off track, but you are playing with God now and that is *not* acceptable. You can go out and act the fool if you want to, but don't play with God, son. This is your soul you're dealing with. You don't want to burn in hell forever." Well, I didn't want to burn in hell forever. But to my way of thinking, hell was what I'd been through before I'd found the Spirit of Truth in Bahá'u'lláh.

One night I got home especially late because I'd cleaned both Dr. Gibson's and the F. C. Pickens' offices after going to a fireside. I slipped into the kitchen to get something to eat. I was hoping that, just this once, maybe I could eat and go right to bed. I prayed, "Oh God, don't let him come bothering me tonight." But I heard Dad get up and walk toward the kitchen. He sat down at the table with his six-inch thick Bible, opened it, and said, "Tell me what you think about this." Then he read: "Jesus said to him, 'I am the way, and the truth, and the life. No one cometh unto the Father but by me.'"[3] When he finished reading, I was amazed to hear myself responding right away. It's hard to describe. My speech was unintentional and uncontrolled. I was a listener even as I talked, and I wondered where the words were coming from.

The essence of what I heard myself say was this—when Jesus says, "No one cometh unto the Father but by me," He is not speaking from a narrow place of ego and one-upmanship. He is speaking from the eternal station of the Manifestation of God, the lifeline between humanity and its Creator yesterday, today, and forever. The Manifestation of God in every era is the way, the truth, and the life.

I gave examples of similar statements from other scripture that, I promise you, I'd never read before. I referred to the Book of Exodus: "Moses alone shall come near the LORD."[4] I pointed out that throughout the Gospel, Jesus confirms the spiritual authority of Moses and claims to fulfill Moses' Cause. Yet the Gospel proclaims that Jesus is the only way to God. "The way to sort out this seeming contradiction," I heard myself explain, "is that both Jesus and Moses were speaking from the same divine realm, stating the necessity of attending to the Word of God."

I quoted Hindu scripture, "Abandoning all duties, come unto Me alone for shelter."[5] I recited words from Buddhism, "This is the path. There is no other that leads to vision."[6] And I quoted other texts that I don't recall. I explained that these apparent claims of exclusivity are not challenges to other stages in the process of progressive Revelation, but different expressions of the same spiritual truth: "All else besides these Manifestations, live by the operation of Their Will, and move and have their being through the out-pourings of Their grace."[7] "This," I finished, "is the Bahá'í understanding of 'Jesus said to him, 'I am the way, and the truth, and the life. No one cometh unto the Father but by me.'" Truly, I didn't know where all my eloquence was coming from, but I did know that everything coming out of my mouth was the truth.

My brother Charles was home from college for the weekend, and he was standing in the doorway listening. When I finished, my father looked at Charles and said, "What do you think of that?" My brother said, "What can I say?" and he walked away. Dad slammed his Bible shut with both hands (I can still hear the "bang!") and left the kitchen, too. I sat there spellbound and thankful for such a wonderful spiritual experience. Because I thought it to be sacred, I didn't mention it to anyone for a long time. About twenty-five years later, I asked Dad if he remembered that night, and he said that he did. I asked him what he remembered, and he said, "I knew it wasn't you doin' the talkin'."

After that night, my father never again came after me with his Bible. Instead, he'd show up with one of my Bahá'í books. He was reading Bahá'í literature with the intent of proving that I was wrong. But in doing so, he was starting on his own path of independent investigation. Previously, I had imagined that if any of my family members were to become Bahá'í, my father would be the last to do so. But now it looked like he'd be the first.

Enrollment

A few weeks passed, and I continued to feel confirmed in the Bahá'í teachings. One night in late November, I was sitting at my bedroom window looking out at the stars, and I asked God to show me a sign confirming that Bahá'u'lláh was the Manifestation of God for this day. The sky always awakened my sense of awe and connection, even when I felt estranged from everything else. But it came to me that, "There will be no fireworks in the sky, no falling stars. You have to look within your heart." I looked in my heart, and I felt sure that Bahá'u'lláh's claim to be the Word of God for this day was true.

Although I was sure that I'd eventually join the Bahá'í community—which, among other things, meant abiding by Bahá'u'lláh's law to abstain from alcohol—and even though I hadn't had a drink in several weeks, something in me wanted to have one last binge before declaring myself as a Bahá'í. So I purchased a half pint of Ancient Age bourbon and hid it away in my closet for an opportune time. Finally, an evening came when I was home alone. I got the bottle out and opened it. As I smelled the bourbon I thought, "I don't need this." I walked to the bathroom and poured it all down the drain.

In order to join the Bahá'í community, I had to be interviewed by a Local Spiritual Assembly. In most churches, a new applicant might be interviewed by a clergyman, but the Bahá'í Faith does not have clergy. It operates with a different administrative system based on a unique process in which Bahá'ís elect governing bodies locally, nationally, and worldwide. A Local Spiritual Assembly is an annually elected governing body that handles the administrative and ministerial affairs of the Bahá'í community within a local legal jurisdiction, such as the city of Greenville.

But there weren't enough Bahá'ís in Greenville to elect a Spiritual Assembly (which requires nine adults), so I made arrangements to be interviewed by the Spiritual Assembly of Augusta, Georgia. If the Assembly determined that I knew enough about the Bahá'í Faith to make an informed decision to join, then I would be granted membership, be able to vote in Bahá'í elections and give to the Fund, and enjoy other privileges of being a member of the Faith. If not, the Assembly would recommend that I continue to study the Faith and apply again in a few months.

My interview was held at the Augusta Bahá'í Center on Kissingbower Road. The center was a small old house behind a private home. It looked like it may have originally been a guesthouse or servants quarters for the larger house in front. I was invited into a small room with the nine Assembly members, some of whom were black and some of whom were white, who introduced themselves and welcomed me warmly.

Mr. Golden, the chairperson, asked all the questions, including "Who is Bahá'u'lláh? What are some of the principles of the Bahá'í Faith? What are the Institutions of the Faith?" He asked about my knowledge of Bahá'í laws and the history of the Faith. Everyone was kind, and I wasn't at all afraid, but I did feel anxious because I wasn't sure if my answers were sufficient. Finally, Mr. Golden asked if I had any questions. There had been one teaching I'd been uneasy about. It had to do with Hinduism.

I liked what I'd learned in the Bahá'í teachings on the spiritual integrity of all the world's major religions. One thing I thought I knew about Hinduism was that Krishna taught that cows were sacred, and that therefore, Hindus didn't eat cows—they worshipped them.

The idea of worshipping cows didn't sit well with me. I had known a few cows. My family had raised cows—some in our backyard. When it came time to slaughter the cow, a friend of ours who was a professional butcher would come over to our house and help my dad with the job in our backyard. Then they'd process the beef right there on our well-covered kitchen table—cut it up into chuck roasts, briskets, short ribs, sirloin steaks, tenderloins, whatever. My job was to help wrap the cut meat in freezer paper, label it, and pack it in our freezer. Now it's true that, while we were raising the cows, they were well cared for. And my mother had this thing where she would not cook and eat the meat from the cow that had just been butchered. She felt too close to it after having helped feed and tend to it up until the time of its slaughter. But she would cook and eat the meat from a cow butchered the year before. That's about as sacred as cows got in our household.

Consequently, I had a hard time believing that cows were ever deserving of special reverence. Of course, I understood that, as a Bahá'í, I would not be expected to follow the Hindu dietary laws. I would follow the laws of Bahá'u'lláh for this day. But it still bothered me, so I asked the Assembly about the sacred cows.

The Assembly members clearly enjoyed the question, but Mr. Golden answered me seriously. He said that there was no way to know exactly what was said thousands of years ago by the Founder of Hinduism, but that we could consider what might have been a practical reason behind this teaching. He suggested that perhaps people were instructed not to eat cows because the cows were needed to pull plows and to produce milk for drinking and for making yoghurt, cheese, and butter. Cows also produced dung, which could be used as fertilizer and dried to make fuel for cooking. In Indian culture, cow dung was also an ingredient in making bricks to build houses. Alive, a cow could be a regular source of milk protein, fat, fertilizer, fuel, and building material for twenty years. "The initial point may have been," Mr. Golden said, "don't eat the factory that sustains you." Over the years, he proposed, maybe this practical dietary law morphed into the belief that cows had some sacred connection to God and were worthy of worship. "The cow," he stated, "certainly is a good symbol for prosperity and the bounty of God." His explanation made sense to me, so the problem of the sacred cows was put to rest. I didn't have any more questions.

I prayerfully waited on the porch while the Assembly consulted. After a short time, I was called back and told that I was accepted as a member of the

Bahá'í Faith. I hugged everybody. That was December 10, 1961, three days before my sixteenth birthday.

Over the next decade, the procedure for enrolling in the Bahá'í community became much more relaxed and enrollment interviews were eventually no longer required. Today, enrollment can happen any time one declares her or his belief in Bahá'u'lláh as the Manifestation of God for today and registers with the national community. The process of studying the history of the Faith and its teachings occurs within the community before as well as after enrollment.

Suspicions

My parents were not surprised that I joined the Bahá'í community. My mother wanted to know more about these people I was spending so much time with, so she asked me to invite some of the Bahá'ís to our house. I invited Eulalia Bobo and Joy Benson. Mom was pleased to meet Eulalia but suspicious of Joy because Joy was white.

Let me explain. Violent and blatant racial injustice was a fact of life in both my and my mother's generations, and it was common knowledge that high on the list of dangers for black men was having anything to do with white women. My mother's earliest childhood memory was a night in 1924 when the Ku Klux Klan came after her Uncle Curt for allegedly whistling at a white woman. The family got word that the Klan would be coming to get Curt, so my Great-Grandmother Sally, who was a no-nonsense woman, made a plan for defense. By the time the Klan got to the house, she had older family members with guns hiding up in trees around the family's little sharecropper house. My then three-year-old mother and her baby sister, Martha, were in the house with their Aunt Corry. The two children were put under a bed for safety. Mom told us that from where she lay, she could hear gunshots and the sound of horses crying in pain. When she darted out from under the bed to go to the horses, Aunt Corry grabbed her arm and threw her back under the bed.

The next day my mother saw that the cotton fields surrounding the house were trampled down and bloodied, but there were no bodies. Uncle Curt was OK but soon left town. Mom didn't know whether or not anyone got killed that night. In those days, when a family member got killed in a racist attack, the older relatives would calmly tell the little children that the person "went away."

I could give you many other examples of how dangerous it was for black men to have any association with white women. The year I was born (1945), one of our immediate neighbors, Hurley Jones, who lived just to the left of us, was executed by the State of South Carolina for fraternizing with a white woman. The two of them had been childhood friends (she lived nearby), and they became "sweethearts" as adults. Their relationship ended when he was electrocuted for the crime of that association under the anti-miscegenation law of South Carolina. At that time, there was no such thing as a consensual relationship between a black man and a white woman, no matter how much the woman wanted and defended the relationship. Hurley's death devastated both families.

Another example: In 1960, the man who lived in the house just to the right of us was beaten senseless for accidentally touching a white woman. He had been shopping at the nearby 8 O'Clock Superette when he slipped on its wet soapy floor. There was a white woman standing near him, and he fell against her. The store called the police. Our neighbor was taken to the police station and beaten senseless. He was never the same after that. He appeared to have suffered severe brain damage from that beating.

Those two incidents were from just one house to the right of us and one house to the left. And these calamities happened in Nicholtown, a "good" neighborhood of business owners and tradesmen. But these are just a few stories of many. A lot of black families went through tragedies caused by racism. The fact was, in order to keep their children alive, black parents had to teach their kids the dos and don'ts of the Deep South. And high on the list of dos for black males was to keep a safe distance from white women.

Then here I come walking into our home with Joy Benson like it was a good idea. Everything my mother knew told her that this situation was a five-alarm fire. She wondered why a young white woman would be interested in associating with black people and what the repercussions might be for the Abercrombie family. My mother was kind to Joy, but there was also a wall of rational concern. Eulalia, however, quickly became a friend of the family.

Penn Center

In January 1962, less than a month after I had joined the Baha'í community, I was invited by Junie Faily (Joy Benson's mother) to my first regional Baha'í winter school. In addition to myself, Junie took her two of her grandchildren and also Helen Strawder (the birthday party Helen). That year, the school was held at Penn Center in the little community of Frogmore on St. Helena Island just off the southern tip of South Carolina, about five hours from Greenville. Junie drove all of us down there in her car.

In 1962, St. Helena was an isolated black-majority island, and Frogmore was not much more than a crossroads with a post office and a small general store. The Penn Center campus was a small collection of buildings with classrooms, a meeting hall, dormitories for men and women, and a kitchen / cafeteria. (Originally called Penn School, it was founded in 1862 by missionaries and abolitionists from Pennsylvania for the purpose of educating freed slaves. As South Carolina progressed in providing more education for blacks, Penn Center changed its focus to serve as a community center and a retreat facility. In 1974, the campus was designated the Penn Center National Historic Landmark District.[8])

The rare quality of Penn Center in 1962 was that it was a large area with good facilities where blacks and whites could meet, study, and enjoy fellowship without harassment from segregationists. The island was not free from segregation, as there were separate beaches for blacks and whites. But happily, one of the Baha'ís had a friend who owned beachfront property, and our integrated groups were welcome to go there.

The Penn Center campus was beautiful. There were a few low white buildings on a broad expanse of land with green everywhere. Old Southern live oaks, with massive branches sweeping almost to the ground, were covered in multileveled canopies of gray Spanish moss. I had never seen anything like it before. I felt like I was in a paradise. The locals who worked at Penn Center were kind, and the food was fantastic.

I had a lot of new experiences at Penn Center. It was the first time I ever tasted Frogmore stew. Also called Low Country boil, it's made out of shrimp, corn, potatoes, sausage, blue crabs, crawfish, and just about anything else you could throw into a pot of spicy boiling water. Once cooked, the stew is drained, all the ingredients are placed on a big platter, and everyone digs in. I learned how to peel crawfish and crabs, and I ate shrimp and grits for the first time. We made friends with the cooks, and two of them investigated the Faith and joined the Bahá'í community later that year.

The setting was beautiful and the food delicious, but the number 1 reason why Penn Center was paradise for me was because it was the first time that I was in the company of dozens of Bahá'ís for days at a time. The school lasted a week, and the fellowship and the spirituality I experienced were different from anything I had known before. I remarked to one of the adults, "Wouldn't it be great if all the Bahá'ís could come together and live in a place like this?" His response was, "That would be nice, but that's not our job. Our job is to make sure that the whole world can enjoy this kind of fellowship."

A lot more people showed up than were expected, so some of us had to sleep on the floor in the dormitory-style sleeping quarters. I volunteered to sleep on the floor, and so did Bill Saunders, a young white man who was in medical school. My bedding was next to his. One night, it had been lights out for some time, but I was still awake, as was Bill. To pass the time, I quietly asked about his plans regarding marriage. Bill whispered back that he hadn't met anybody that fit all of the qualities that he was looking for in a woman. "What qualities are you looking for?" I asked. Bill named several virtues such as kindness, forgiveness, courage, and generosity. I admired him for wanting all those attributes in a spouse. But then he whispered, "And she has to be black." Surprised, I whispered back, "But Bill, what if you don't find all those qualities in a black woman, but you do find them in a white woman?" He whispered, "Then I won't get married." Now his attitude, I thought, was not in the spirit of the oneness of humanity. Why would he even consider the color of a woman's skin? To my mind, his thinking was backward and, well, satanic. So, I whispered back, "Bill, that's like the Devil wanting to marry the Virgin Mary." Everybody in the dormitory, who we thought had been sound asleep, erupted into loud laughter!

I didn't see or hear from Bill for the next fifteen years. Then one day I got a letter from "Dr. Bill Saunders" and it said, "Dear Ricky, The devil asked the Virgin Mary to marry him and she said, 'Yes.' *Alláh-u-Abhá!*" That's all he wrote. (*Alláh-u-Abhá* is an Arabic expression meaning "God is most glorious!")

One of the school sessions was a celebration of the fiftieth anniversary of 'Abdu'l-Bahá's visit to the United States (1911–1912). 'Abdu'l-Bahá was the eldest son of Bahá'u'lláh and in every way a significant figure to Bahá'ís. A large picture of 'Abdu'l-Bahá was featured at the front of the meeting room. I was there when Mrs. Chaplain, an elderly lady who lived on St. Helena Island and who had come for the first time to find out what these Bahá'ís were about, walked into the room, looked at the picture of 'Abdu'l-Bahá, gasped loudly, put her hand to her heart, and said, "I've seen Him before!" She shared that when she was a little girl, she was with her mother at a railroad station in New York when she saw 'Abdu'l-Bahá get off of one of the trains. She had felt drawn to Him, but her mother wouldn't let her approach Him. Mrs. Chaplain was thrilled to finally be "meeting" 'Abdu'l-Bahá at this program. He had left an impression on her that had lasted over fifty years. After investigating the Faith, she enrolled in the Bahá'í community

When the school was over and we were driving back to Greenville, we stopped at a diner in Sumter to eat. By the beginning of 1962 there were a few integrated restaurants, and we were hoping this diner was one of them. As we walked in the door, the waitress took one look at us, then ran to the back of the restaurant and disappeared behind a door. Then the manager came out shouting, "You can't eat here, you can't come in here, get out!" We were about to leave when Junie turned back around and asked the manager, "Can't we at least get something for the children?" He snapped back, "No, get out." So, we left.

Just as we were getting into her car, Junie told us that because that man had been so unkind, she was going to give him a piece of her mind. Now you have to understand that Junie was an angel. I had never seen an angel get mad before, and I had no idea what she was going to do. As she was making her way across the parking lot to the diner, I got real nervous about her safety. I got out of the car and caught up with her just as she opened the restaurant door.

Inside, the manager was standing there talking to the waitress. Junie pointed at him and in all of her five-foot, ninety-pound, silver-haired fury said, "I don't think you're very nice!" I thought, "Is that *it*?" Then she turned around and walked back to the car. We all got in and rode off. She had told the man off in her angelic way.

- 5 -

"You Get Off That Tractor"

It was the middle of January 1962 and I was joyously lugging Eulalia's two suitcases up our long staircase to one of our spare rooms. Mom and Eulalia had become best of friends and, knowing that Eulalia was here from out of town, Mom had invited her to stay with us for the rest of her time in Greenville. Our house had eight bedrooms, so it was easy for us to accommodate houseguests and provide them with their own private rooms. I was thrilled about this new development not only because Eulalia was a lot of fun to be around, but also because—at least for a while—I would not be the only Bahá'í living at 8 Rebecca Street! We all got along great—so much so that Dad felt comfortable enough to subject Eulalia to the inquisitions that he had previously directed at me. But before I tell you about the religious discussions between my father and Eulalia, let me share a few more things about my dad.

It seemed that everybody in Greenville knew my father because he had done construction work just about everywhere. He was well-respected by both black and white folks alike. Back in the day, our neighborhood was full of tradesmen, but most were exploited. They couldn't get their own construction licenses (such as carpentry, masonry, or plumbing licenses) because they were black, so they had to get jobs working under white contractors and were often poorly treated and badly compensated. But Dad was licensed as a brick mason and as a building contractor, and he was known among the tradesmen for fair treatment of his hired help. He was also known by everyone for his excellent work and high standards. He was a master craftsman who took pride in the fact that every job was done right. Dad was quick to let people know that if they didn't want to listen to him or trust his judgment about the best way to do a job, they could do the work themselves.

In addition, Dad would not tolerate disrespect of any kind on his worksites. One particular occasion comes to mind. It was the summer of 1959. Dad had a contract to build homes on the Bob Jones University campus in Greenville. My brother Charles and I were two of eight workers that Dad hired for the job of moving in building materials and preparing the site for construction. Charles and I were teenagers but the other workers were grown men. Of course, we were all black. One of the Bob Jones employees, a white man, had been assigned by the university to scrape and even out the site with a school tractor. He did most of the scraping, but he had come about five feet short on one long side next to a big building. We noticed that he was driving the tractor away from the site as if he had finished his work. That meant the eight of us would have to dig and even out that long strip of land with picks and shovels, a hard job that could be done in a fraction of the time by just one man on a tractor. So, my father flagged down the white guy on the tractor and asked him to finish the work. In response, the white guy pointed to the eight of us and shouted out, "Get them boys out there to do it." Dad coldly answered, "The only 'boys' out there are my two sons."

My father couldn't tolerate grown men being called "boys." It had long been a practice of prejudiced white people to call black men "boys" instead of "men," thereby attempting to undermine the black men's identities as adults deserving of respect. But after Dad corrected him, the guy pointed again to all eight of us workers and said, "Let them boys take them picks and shovels and do it."

At that point, my father told the white guy to get off the tractor. We froze. Black men didn't tell white men what to do. And we were keenly aware of the significance of the work site, Bob Jones University. Bob Jones, Sr., the head of that university, was an outspoken and powerful opposer of civil rights and promoter of white supremacy.

The guy on the tractor objected to my father's demand. Dad told him again, "You get off that tractor." The man didn't move. Then my father jumped up on the tractor, grabbed the guy by the arm, "helped" him off the tractor, and told him to leave. The white guy walked away at a pretty good speed. The eight of us figured we were all dead.

Dad had never driven that particular kind of tractor before, but he quickly figured out how to shift the gears and work the levers. He set the blade and got that tractor to do what he wanted it to do. He finished the scraping in ten minutes. The job would have taken the eight of us at least three hours. Then he asked us how it looked. We told him it was good. He said, "OK, I'm gonna take that man his tractor back." My brother Charles said, "No, Daddy, don't go down there." We were all scared that the white guy might be waiting on my dad with a gun. Dad said, "No, I've done what I needed to do. I'm gonna take the man his tractor back." He was gone just a little while, and then we saw him walking back toward us with the tractor guy at his side.

The tractor guy walked up to the eight of us and asked, "What kind of drinks y'all want from the store?"

His sudden hospitality and concern for our welfare was bizarre. We didn't know what to say, so we all shook our heads and said, "Nothin'." Even Doc and Willy, who were always hungry, said, "Nothin'."

Then Dad spoke up saying, "Y'all tell the man what you want."

Since Dad said it, we went ahead and told the guy what we wanted: RC Cola, Pepsi, Orange, Grape, Upper Ten, whatever.

The white guy left and came back with not just eight drinks but with a whole wooden case of sodas, twenty-four in all. And he had bought other snacks for us, as well—crackers, chips, and candy bars. He was polite for the rest of the time we were out on that job. We just shook our heads. My brother Charles speculated that Dad had caused that man to have a significant emotional and spiritual breakthrough. That's the kind of man my dad was.

I guess it was about a week or so after Eulalia moved in when Dad initiated the first religious debate with our new houseguest. It was a school night and a couple of hours after dinner. The youngest Abercrombies (Sherry, Beverly, and Phillip) were in bed. Eulalia, Mom, Dad, and my older brother Harold and I were at the kitchen table finishing off a sweet potato pie when Dad just up and asked Eulalia, "How do the Bahá'ís do baptism?" Eulalia replied, "Well, Mr. Abercrombie, let's find out." She got out a Bahá'í book—*Some*

Answered Questions—and read a few passages stating that baptism was a symbol of repentance, that true repentance is a virtue and a blessing and necessary for the purification of the soul, and that the symbolic ritual of baptism with water is not required in the Dispensation of Bahá'u'lláh.

Dad was a deacon at Tabernacle Baptist Church. He objected to what he heard from Eulalia and argued that baptism by water was necessary for salvation. He left the kitchen and came back with a Bible. Eulalia did the same.

And it was on.

Dad read a verse having to do with baptism by water and insisted that was all there was to be said. Eulalia read a different verse, the one where John the Baptist says that he baptizes with water, but the One Who came after him would baptize with the Holy Spirit and with fire.[1]

"How many people you seen baptized by fire?" she asked.

"Well, you can't take that literally," said my dad.

Eulalia agreed and asked, "So why take 'water' literally?" She shared the Bahá'í teachings on the spiritual meaning of "fire" and "water" in those verses.

Dad insisted that "water" had to be taken literally, and the debate continued.

Somewhere during their argument I'd noticed that Harold had disappeared. I was eyeing the door myself. I finally slipped out and went upstairs to bed. But I didn't get much sleep. There was a new sound in the house. Loud debate. Eulalia would begin to state a point, then Dad would interrupt in a louder voice about how those Bahá'í teachings were false. Eulalia would respond with whatever volume was necessary to complete her statement. It was a novel experience for me to hear Dad argue loudly. When I was the subject of his inquisitions the conversation was intense but not loud. I knew better than to raise my voice to my father, or to interrupt him. Occasionally, Mom and Dad might disagree and discuss their different opinions on this or that matter, but never did they raise their voices. I figure Dad was doing what he felt he had to do to protect his own. He probably thought that discrediting Eulalia, my main Bahá'í teacher, was his chance to save my soul. Dad brought up a dozen doctrinal issues, and the debate continued until about two o'clock in the morning. The next night and the night after, the same thing happened—only the debates began earlier and lasted longer. Mother provided coffee for as long as they needed it.

My father was large and powerful with an exceptionally strong personality. I would describe Eulalia the same way. You've probably heard of Joe Louis, the legendary world heavyweight boxing champion? Well, Eulalia happened to be Joe Louis's younger sister. Really. His blood sister. Joe Louis and Eulalia looked so much alike you would have thought they were twins. She was tall, strong, and stood eye-to-eye with my dad. Eulalia and Dad matched each other not only in size but also in energy, eloquence, strength of conviction, and knowledge of the Bible. Whatever attitude my father brought, Eulalia brought it, too. When they were debating, it was as if two tigers had entered the same small space. Emotional sparks flew, and lampshades shook with the volume of their voices. I generally kept my distance, as did everybody else. We didn't *have* to be in the room to hear what they were talking about.

Although the arguments were fierce, I wouldn't say they were uncivil. Eulalia and Dad both had strong opinions and they expressed them vigorously. But when they weren't in the middle of a debate, they'd be just as polite as the rest of us and showed no animosity.

I Have Wrestled

It was the beginning of the second week of debates when I heard Dad say to Eulalia, "If you would just be quiet for five minutes, I could teach you something." She replied, "OK, Mr. Abercrombie, I will be quiet and let you talk for five minutes. Then you be quiet and let *me* talk for five minutes." I was in the kitchen with Mom and I could see that she was trying to contain her laughter over these new rules of engagement.

The arguments continued, but Eulalia and Dad stuck to their five-minute rule. Things quieted down and there seemed to be more listening going on. The evenings ended earlier, too. I don't think that was because of a reduced energy about religion, though. I think they ended earlier because both probably felt that they were killing themselves from lack of sleep. After a week or so of orderly communication, I noticed my father's focus on debate had transformed into a sincere desire to learn more about Bahá'u'lláh and His teachings. What had been debate matches turned into study sessions. Dad was showing appreciation for Eulalia's guidance as she pointed him to the Bahá'í writings related to his questions. Mom joined their study (she'd kept her distance from the fiery debates, as I had), and the three of them laughed a lot.

I think the teaching that most grabbed Dad's attention, first in an agitated way and ultimately in an enthusiastic way, was the principle of progressive Revelation. With time, reading, and study, Dad came to rejoice in the concept that all of the Founders of the world's great religions came from the same Source, taught the same foundational truths for the same purpose, and brought social teachings specific to the age in which They appeared. They represented the same Light in different Lamps. Dad was particularly interested in the connection between the Revelations of Jesus Christ and Bahá'u'lláh. The following passage from *'Abdu'l-Baha in London* especially caught his attention: "A friend asked how the teachings of Bahá'u'lláh contrasted with the teachings of Jesus Christ. 'The teachings are the same,' declared 'Abdu'l-Bahá; 'It is the same foundation and the same temple. Truth is one, and without division. The teachings of Jesus are in a concentrated form. Men do not agree to this day as to the meaning of many of His sayings. His teachings are as a flower in the bud. Today, the bud is unfolding into a flower! Bahá'u'lláh has expanded and fulfilled the teachings, and has applied them in detail to the whole world.'"[2]

Maybe it was because Dad was a brick mason and building contractor that the idea of different religious systems progressively built on the same foundation for a common purpose especially appealed to him. Or maybe the comparison of Christ's teachings to a bud now unfolding into the flower of the Bahá'í Revelation spoke to the farmer in him who loved to plant seeds and watch plants grow. Whatever the reason, Dad was inspired by the above quote and, in February of 1962, he set out to find the answer to this particular question: How *does* Bahá'u'lláh's Revelation expand and fulfill the teachings of Christ? I could see Eulalia helping him some, but this question was clearly his project, and he worked on it for weeks.

Dad found what he was looking for and shared his learnings with us over many dinners—"us" being Mom, me, my big brother Harold, my younger siblings Sherry, Beverly, and Phillip, and whoever else might be at the table, family or not. "Bahá'u'lláh has magnified, clarified, and applied Christ's teachings on unity and love," Dad would say, "and thank God He has, because folks have either ignored, misunderstood, changed, or forgotten them, and the world's the worse for it."

The proofs Dad gave that the Bahá'í Faith magnified Christ's teachings included Bahá'u'lláh's declaration that all of the people of the earth are spiritually one, and that prejudice of any kind is a spiritual disease. He saw Bahá'u'lláh's call for a universal auxiliary language, a world tribunal, a world currency, and universal education as modern expressions of Christ's call for love and unity. I could go on, but essentially, Dad saw every teaching and ordinance of Bahá'u'lláh as needful for mankind to realize the Kingdom of God on Earth as prophesied in the Lord's Prayer. And Dad accepted Bahá'u'lláh as the Manifestation of God for today.

My father didn't officially join the Bahá'í community at this time. He said he wanted to study more, especially about the Bahá'í Administrative Order, before being eligible to be elected to serve on a Local Spiritual Assembly. But both he and Mom started attending firesides at the Bensons' and the Shumates', and they continued their study of the Faith with Eulalia at home. In appreciation of Eulalia's patience, resilience, and wisdom in teaching, Dad would say, "I have wrestled with the Angel Gabriel. And the angel has won." Sometime later, I asked Eulalia why she hadn't just bailed out of our house when my dad was so adamant about challenging the Faith. She said, "There's no way I was going to abandon you, Ricky."

It was pure joy to engage in the study of the Faith with my parents. Harold, Beverly, and often Della and her husband joined us as well. I could freely share the best part of myself with my family, the people I loved the most. My dad's determination to discredit the Faith had transformed into a determination to teach the Faith, so he arranged to host a fireside at our home where he would be the presenter. He invited everyone he had met at the Bensons' and Shumates' firesides *and* all of the members of Tabernacle Baptist Church.

The evening of the fireside, our living room was full of people, including a few folks from Tabernacle Baptist. There was overflow seating in the adjoining foyer and up the stairs. And there was my dad, looking ten feet tall. He started by inviting prayers and then gave a brief introduction to some of Bahá'u'lláh's teachings. When he got to the principle of progressive Revelation, he brought out several drinking glasses and lined them up on the coffee table. Each was different. Some were tall and clear, others had designs, and some were coffee mugs. They were all empty.

Dad poured water from a pitcher into the first cup and said, "Imagine that this water is the Word of God that inspires, sustains, and educates humanity. And imagine that this cup is the religion of Abraham. Abraham was the Word of God Who taught people the oneness of God." When the Abraham cup was full, he picked it up and poured its water into a second cup. "Now this water is the same Word of God that appeared through Abraham, but now it is appearing in the Revelation of Moses. Moses taught a lot of laws because civilization had advanced, and the people were ready for them." He continued like this—always pouring the same water into the next cup—until he had included all of the major religions leading up to the Bahá'í Faith.

"The point," he explained, "is that the Word of God in every Revelation has the same spiritual substance and purpose—to inspire, sustain, and educate humanity to an ever-advancing civilization. But the 'cups' or religions looked different because the teachings and laws of the Manifestations of God address the different needs and capacities of different times." Then he poured the water into the last cup, the Bahá'í Faith. "Bahá'u'lláh has brought the same water, the Word of God that guided humanity in the past, and He has applied this Word to our time. If you're thirsty for the Word of God for this Day, which cup would you drink from?"

I was so proud that he was my father! His demonstration made progressive Revelation of the Word of God so clear—the same spiritual substance appearing in different laws and ordinances suited to different times. The Bahá'ís in the room, and those who had been investigating the Faith, appreciated the clarity of his explanation. Eulalia was beside herself. Dad had surprised us all with his analogy. The minister and friends who came from Tabernacle Baptist Church were clearly disturbed, and they didn't stay too long when we broke for refreshments. Mom and Dad were still glowing much later that evening when I finally got to bed.

Not Negotiable

By mid-March of 1962, my parents were hosting regular firesides and advertising them in the Greenville newspaper: "Bahá'í Fireside every Saturday night at 8 Rebecca Street, the home of Charles Abercrombie." A few of my classmates started coming. One of the great things about firesides at our house was the music. Harold and Beverly were particularly gifted in inspiring our friends through song. We had a piano in our living room. Mother initially got it for Della in the hopes that she would learn to play, but Della was more interested in playing football and baseball than in playing the piano. When Harold was old enough to play around with it, he sounded pretty good, so Mother got him signed up for lessons. He took one lesson and wouldn't go back because the teacher taught too slowly. Instead, he taught himself how to play the piano as well as to read and write music. Harold was a lot like my grandfather, John Willie; he could do pretty much anything he wanted to do. Not only did Harold enhance our firesides and raise our spirits with amazing music, he also went on to become a professional singer / piano player. Beverly was born with the voice of an angel, and we always called upon her to sing.

Like other Bahá'í meetings, these firesides were integrated groups. And like what happened at the Bensons', the police would usually show up outside our house. They'd park right in our driveway and sit there for five, ten, fifteen minutes as people were arriving and also during the meeting. Sometimes they would knock on the door and ask what we were selling or what we were drinking. We'd always invite them inside, but they never would come in the house. But by the end of that year, the police stopped showing up at our firesides, and they didn't go to the Bensons' anymore, either. At most, they'd drive past the house and wave.

As my mother got to know Joy and Junie and other Bahá'í women, she was able to detach from her fears about her family having associations with white women—at least, in a Bahá'í setting. That was something that I had to keep reminding myself of, as well. As a person of color, I found that there was the danger of thinking that the same feelings of fellowship and respect that existed among the black and white Bahá'ís existed in the community at large. It didn't. Even today, I still have to remind myself of this sad reality for my own safety.

Mom and Junie became the best of friends, and Joy was like a daughter to her. Junie taught Bahá'í spiritual education classes for Joy's children—Mark, Lane, and David—along with my younger siblings, Sherry, Phillip, and Beverly. Sometimes Junie would hold the classes at the Bensons' home and sometimes at our house. The kids loved those classes. When people would ask my little brother Phillip what he wanted to be when he grew up he'd say, "I want to be an *Alláh-u-Abhá* preacher!"

Although Bahá'ís don't have "preachers" in the sense of professional clergy (Bahá'u'lláh gave His followers a different way to administer the affairs of the community), I have to say that Phillip did, in his own way, become an "*Alláh-u-Abhá* preacher." As a young couple, he and his wife, Dorcus, provided spiritual education to virtually all of the young people who lived in their community, the Laurel Creek area of Greenville. Wherever Phillip and Dorcus went, those kids went, too. The neighborhood kids were like their own kids. And over the years, Dorcus and Phillip have continued to provide guidance, spiritual education, and nurturing to children, both in the Bahá'í community and in the greater community. While they never had biological children of their own, there are dozens of children, youth, and adults—of all ethnicities—who call Phillip and Dorcus their spiritual parents or grandparents.

On one side of the Bensons' yard, there was a bit of a slope where the Bensons had made a slip and slide—that is, a long sheet of plastic that the kids would spray with water and slide down. This was one of many games that the Bahá'í children played in the Bensons' yard. Several of the Bensons' neighbors told them that white children should not be playing with colored children. But their neighbors' opinions didn't change the way the Bensons did things. They remained focused on living up to Bahá'u'lláh's teachings on race unity.

My father was now enthusiastically telling everyone he knew about Bahá'u'lláh. He'd introduce the Faith in a type of language he felt the people would understand. More than once, he announced to the congregation of Tabernacle Baptist that the Spirit of Christ had returned in the glory of the Father and that His new name was Bahá'u'lláh. His proclamations created quite a stir. I'm told that news about Daddy's interest in the Faith spread like wildfire throughout the black community. My classmate Smitty told me that he often heard his older relatives comment, "Lord, I don't know what happened. Charles Abercrombie? Those Bahá'ís done got him, too."

People thought that my parents had some sort of mental breakdown or something. They couldn't figure out how Mom and Dad could separate themselves from the church so quickly. My parents were regularly confronted wih challenges to their religious interest. Dad and I were walking out of the Winn Dixie grocery store one afternoon when he was accosted in the parking lot by Mr. Williams. The conversation went like this:

Mr. Williams: "I hear you joined the Bahá'ís."

Dad: "That's right."

Mr. Williams: "Where's the Bahá'í church?"

Dad: "The Bahá'ís don't have a building."

Mr. Williams: "Where do y'all meet?"

Dad: "In our homes."

Mr. Williams: "Where's the Bahá'í cemetery?"

Dad: "There's no Bahá'í cemetery in Greenville."

Mr. Williams: "What about the choir?"

Dad: "There's no Bahá'í choir in Greenville, but we sing a lot."

Mr. Williams: "Who's the preacher?"

Dad: "Bahá'ís don't have preachers.

Mr. Williams: "Then who tells you what to do?"

Dad: "We have the writings of Bahá'u'lláh, the Word of God for this day."

Mr. Williams: "Why don't you believe in Jesus anymore?"

Dad: "I do believe in Jesus. Jesus is my Lord and Savior. That's not negotiable. And to follow my Lord and Savior today, I am following Bahá'u'lláh."

Mr. Williams: "How you gonna like joining some church that ain't got no church, no cemetery, no choir, and no preacher?"

Dad: "Where does Christ say that His followers are going to like everything that comes their way on the path to salvation?"

So ended that little interaction.

Although most of their friends and associates could not see the new Revelation of the Word of God, Mom and Dad continued to follow their hearts. Mr. Williams remained friends with my father but always tried to convince Dad that he was going to hell for believing in Bahá'u'lláh. Dad was undaunted and continued to enjoy Mr. Williams' friendship. It would be a hard call to determine who prayed for the other the most.

Although Dad had received a cold reception at Tabernacle Baptist, this rejection did not prevent him from sharing the news of Bahá'u'lláh with other congregations. He made it a habit to visit churches on Sundays with his good news. This is what he did: In most black churches (at least at that time) there was a period before or during the service when the preacher or some other church official asked all visitors to stand, introduce themselves, and say a few words. My father would arrive as a visitor and when asked to introduce himself he would say, "I'm Charles Abercrombie, and I just want to tell you this morning that y'all are waiting for Christ to return but He already has." Then he'd sit down. After church, people would come up and ask Dad about that, and he'd give them a short lesson on the Bahá'í Faith. Whenever he made these church visits, he wasn't looking to convert anybody, he was just looking to proclaim the Faith. He'd say, "You don't make Bahá'ís, you find them."

I went with Dad to a church one Sunday when he did his usual declaration. Outside afterward, one of the men came up, pointed to the church graveyard, and said, "I don't see nobody raisin' from the dead." The lack of dead bodies coming to life was meant as proof that Christ had not returned. Dad said, "People been dyin' a long time. If they start raisin' up and walkin' the earth, where we gonna put *you?*" He went on to explain the spiritual meaning of that prophecy, and we talked to several folks for a long time that afternoon.

- 6 -

Strange Looks

One of my gambling acquaintances caught up with me in the school hallway. "Fourth period, Rick, poker at Fred's. See you there," he said quietly. I quickly responded with "Sorry, can't make it." "Hold it," he said as he grabbed my arm. He swung around, faced me straight on, looked at me like I was crazy, and asked, "What's been goin' on with you, man? Who *are* you?"

I knew why he was upset. Up to a few months ago, I had been a member of a group of five or six guys who regularly cut classes in order to gamble with cards or dice. One of the group, Fred, lived across the street from Sterling High School. We'd cut class, slip across the street for a few games at Fred's house (unbeknown to his parents who were both at work), and then get back to school in time for the next class period. We rotated the classes that we missed so as not to draw too much attention to our activity, and would usually do this gambling outing once a week or so. But for months (since the weekend of my first Bahá'í fireside) I'd been opting out of gambling as well as truancy. Now my friend was demanding that I explain this outrageous new law-abiding behavior.

I actually got this kind of question a lot—from teenagers I knew and even some I didn't know. They noticed how I'd changed and they wanted to know how and why I became a different person. Funny, it hadn't been hard for me to change, but it was hard for people to accept that I had crossed from drunkenness and delinquency into respect and responsibility. Although it seemed like most of my classmates were not interested in religion, all I could do was tell them the truth about how I was recreated. It was all about Bahá'u'lláh.

A few friends became curious and began investigating the Faith along with me. But for most of my cohorts, the initial response was skepticism, strange looks, and joking.

With my desire to be involved in healthy activities, I had joined the high school track team. This athleticism was new for me. I learned that our school had a program where athletes got free lunches once a week in the cafeteria during the season when their sport was being played. Well, now it was track season, but it was also the month of March, which is a time of fasting for Bahá'ís age fifteen and older. By fasting, I mean that Bahá'ís who are physically able don't eat or drink from sunup to sundown for a period of nineteen days. So, there I was in the cafeteria with all of my teammates, and they were grabbing their free lunches. But I didn't grab a lunch because I was fasting. They asked me, "Hey Ricky, why don't you get your lunch?" I said, "I'm fasting." They were like, "You're doing what?!"

Fasting was not a part of the religious culture of any of my classmates at Sterling High School. Virtually all of the students there were Baptist or AME (African Methodist Episcopal). None of them fasted, and my teammates didn't know what I was talking about. I explained, "I'm a Bahá'í, and we fast." Their response was what I had grown used to: "You're what? What are you talking about?" So, I continued, as I always did. "Yes, the Word of God has returned, His new name is Bahá'u'lláh, and we are living at the beginning of a new era in the Cause of God." They responded, as was typical, with an incredulous "What?" But they really didn't want to know "what." Then came the joking: "Rick's been drinking too much wine or something. He's lost his mind!" Lots of laughter. I didn't mind the joking. I'd had a notoriously errant past, and I'd done some crazy stuff. But now all I had was my truth.

Cost of Oneness

I got teased a lot by my friends because of my new religious interest, but I came to find out that this good-natured kidding was nothing compared to the hostilities that had been experienced by the adults in the Greenville Bahá'í community for years. In addition to religious prejudice, these hostilities came about because of the Faith's association with integration. The principle of the oneness of humanity is embedded in the scripture of the Bahá'í Faith along with spiritual and social teachings on the many implications of this truth. For example, Bahá'u'lláh clearly forbade slavery. In His Book of Laws He states, "It is forbidden you to trade in slaves, be they men or women. Let no man exalt himself above another. . . ."[1] To my understanding, Bahá'u'lláh was the first Manifestation of God to establish such a law. Racial prejudice is named in Bahá'í scripture as one of the evils capable of destroying the foundations of humanity, and the realization of race unity is identified as a prerequisite for world peace.[2] Since the beginning of the Faith, Bahá'ís have worked toward the goal of integrated communities, and I was witnessing the fruit of those efforts in the Bahá'í gatherings I attended.* This integration and close association was a great bounty to me, as it was to others.

However, living out the Bahá'í teachings on the oneness of humanity came at a cost. The experience of Virginia Ford comes to mind. Virginia, a white woman, was one of the first Greenville natives to join the Bahá'í community. Virginia lived on Maco Terrace—at that time a street in a white neighborhood near Nicholtown. A decade or so earlier, the Ku Klux Klan had burned a cross in Virginia's front yard and bashed in the windows of her house—all because she welcomed black people into her home. She continued to teach the Faith and participate in its activities.** Many years later, after houses on Maco Terrace had been mostly bought out by black people, Virginia's new black neighbors harassed her with comments like, "You better get out of here, white lady. This is a black neighborhood." It was ever so frustrating for Virginia.

The Bensons had experienced hostilities as well. After I came to know Joy and Dick, I learned that they had moved to Greenville in 1956 right after getting married. They had both completed their educations in their home state of Michigan. Joy was a medical doctor (an unusual achievement for a woman

---

* For more information on the growth of the Bahá'í Faith in South Carolina, see Venters, *No Jim Crow Church.*

** For more information on the life of Virginia Ford, see Venters, *No Jim Crow Church,* pp. 158, 179, 188–89, 216.

at that time) and Dick had just graduated from law school. Joy was a member of the Bahá'í community; Dick was not. They were both interested in settling someplace in South Carolina, so they drove around the state looking for the place they would like to call home. Both were attracted to Greenville. Dick was recruited by a prestigious law firm in Greenville, but the job didn't work out because of his association with Bahá'ís.

When Dick was interviewed at the law firm office, they offered him a job as an attorney right away, and they arranged for him to come back the next day to sign the contract and do all the paperwork involved with taking on that employment. But before he left the office, Dick asked to use the office telephone to call Joy and share the good news. Now because Dick and Joy had just come to Greenville, they were staying at the home of a Greenville Bahá'í, Grace van der Heydt. Dick didn't have Grace's phone number on him, so he asked the office secretary to find Grace van der Heydt in the phone book. Someone asked Dick how he knew Grace, and he freely shared that he knew Grace because Joy, his wife, was a Bahá'í. It was obvious that everyone in the room took notice. When Dick returned to the office the next day to sign the contract and finish the paperwork, nobody would talk to him. He sat there for two hours, ignored. He finally left. Over the next few months of job searching, it became obvious that Dick had been blacklisted by all the other law firms in Greenville. No one would hire him, regardless of his excellent credentials. He finally secured a part-time position searching real estate titles at a law firm owned by a man named George Townes. George's wife, Laura, was a Quaker, so George was a little more broad-minded.

After living in Greenville for a couple of years, during which time he did his own investigation of the Bahá'í teachings, Dick joined the Bahá'í community. Eventually, he opened his own legal office, and even though he was white, he chose to rent a space in an office building that housed black businesses. He also hired a black secretary. Both of these things were unheard of in the South.

I admired how Dick used his legal expertise to serve the Faith. For example, early in 1961, some months before I met him, Dick spearheaded an effort by South Carolina Bahá'ís' to appeal to the state of South Carolina in order to get official state recognition for the Bahá'í marriage service, a simple ceremony that requires the presence of two witnesses approved by the Local Spiritual Assembly. The request was granted, making it legal for Spiritual Assemblies to officiate marriages in South Carolina, just like ministers and rabbis. This legal recognition opened the way for the Bahá'ís of Greenville to apply for and achieve incorporation as a religious organization in South Carolina.

Joy's professional journey was a little different. She was able to secure a job as an intern at Greenville Hospital shortly after she and Dick moved to Greenville. Her position was especially fortunate because it enabled her and Dick to lease one of the hospital-owned rental houses (for medical staff), which was quite affordable. The house was located close to the hospital in a racially borderline neighborhood where it was common to see both black and white people on the street. An advantage of this neutral location was that whenever Joy and Dick invited black people to their home, it was not very noticeable, so neither their guests or their household would get harassed by segregationists.

Joy shared with me that during her internship, pretty much the only negative experience she had was with supervising doctors who objected to her bedside manner. The problem was that she persisted in addressing all male patients who were older than her as "Mister . . . ." even if they were men of color. The doctor accompanying her on her rounds would chastise her whenever she'd do that and say, for example, "You should have just called him Jim." Nevertheless, she successfully completed her internship.

But in the late 1950s, when she got pregnant with their first child, Joy had to stop working. At that time, pregnancy was considered highly unacceptable in any professional setting and absolutely unthinkable for a doctor. Because she had to resign from her medical job, she and Dick had to move out of hospital housing. With the help of Joy's parents (Junie and John Faily, who came from Michigan to live with Joy and Dick) they purchased a large two-story house in the white Overbrook neighborhood in the heart of Greenville. Their house was the site of my first Bahá'í fireside in 1961.

The whiteness of the Overbrook neighborhood did not make it easy for the Bensons and Failys to host Bahá'í meetings. Some of their neighbors made it clear that they objected to the integrated nature of the groups that Joy and Dick welcomed into their home. One elderly woman who lived in the house right next door would often become inebriated, sit on her screened-in front porch, and yell out obscenities at the Bensons' guests. She was most active during firesides. As blacks and whites alike walked into the Benson's house, this neighbor would get to hollering and cussing so loud that everybody up and down the street could hear her. I couldn't understand why she wasn't arrested for disturbing the peace. I secretly thought it might be a good idea to throw a brick in her direction. When asked about that neighbor's behavior, Junie Faily would always say, "We have to pray for her." I thought, "What a reply!"

About six months after I started attending the Bensons' firesides, that particular neighbor died, and a different elderly neighbor lady decided that she needed to take up screaming at the Bensons' guests. When she passed away several months later, a third elderly woman in the neighborhood took up the post. After a year or so, she also passed away, and fireside nights were a good bit quieter.

In addition to the unwanted vocal attention of some of the neighbors, the Bensons also received threatening phone calls. Rumors flew that the Bensons ran an illegal gambling ring and that they were otherwise lawless troublemakers. One of their neighbors happened to be a state legislator, and he took a petition to the General Assembly stating that the Bensons were communists who participated in illegal integration activities. Police would park in front of the Bensons' home, shine spotlights on peoples' faces as they came and went, and write down the license plate numbers of the guests' cars. I don't know if the police attention discouraged anybody from going to the Bensons' gatherings, but it didn't discourage me. It also didn't discourage some of the other neighbors who became curious about the Bensons' social and religious ideas, admired the Bensons for their beliefs, and became lifelong friends.

Social Suicide

My parents' association with the Bahá'í community brought them the bounty of new friends and an increasingly rich spiritual life, but it also brought loss and complications. Many people who had previously been friends (or at least friendly) abandoned or acted out against our family. Reverend Watson of Tabernacle Baptist Church told my parents that they were going to hell and that they wouldn't be able to find anybody to bury them since they'd affiliated with this "radical" religion. Folks who used to be regular visitors to our house no longer stopped by, and social groups that my mom and dad had been involved with no longer included them in their gatherings. Mom had hosted a weekly sewing group for years, but as soon as word got around that she was associated with the Bahá'ís, all those ladies stopped coming to the house. Just about every friend of my parents—not all, but most—bailed out on them. This religious prejudice was something we'd never experienced before.

Of Daddy's twelve siblings, only two of them, Lee Marion (Uncle Lee) and Richard Floyd ("Duck"), took the time to actually investigate the Bahá'í Faith on their own. Both of them eventually declared as Bahá'ís. Uncle Clifton (one of Dad's older brothers) actually forbade his family to associate with us altogether. It was sad. Dad and Uncle Cliff had been like twins—they both did masonry work, taught masonry at vocational centers, loved to grow things, and had kids in the same age range. Uncle Cliff had always looked up to my father, even though Uncle Cliff was two years older than Dad. My siblings and I used to go to Uncle Cliff's home in Spartanburg and stay for a week or two at a time during school vacations. But all that visiting stopped when Dad started telling people about Bahá'u'lláh.

The estrangement between Dad and Uncle Cliff lasted for over twenty years. Then, around 1985, Uncle Cliff's wife, Aunt Nancy, had a disabling stroke. She couldn't do any cooking, so she asked Uncle Cliff to bring her to our house to eat sometimes because she remembered that she especially liked Momma's cooking. Of course, they were welcome. But at first when they'd come, Aunt Nancy would eat, but Uncle Cliff wouldn't. He'd help her if she needed help, but he wouldn't eat. Neither would he engage in dinner conversation. Meanwhile, we would attend to Aunt Nancy and be as hospitable as we could. After several of these visits, Uncle Cliff began to eat a few bites, and he and Daddy would talk some. Eventually, Uncle Cliff joined us in eating meals and in all of our conversations. Dad and Uncle Cliff's relationship grew more cordial over time. Their amiability was possible because the two of them had a silent agreement that they wouldn't talk about religion. But it took over twenty years to get to that agreement.

In addition to loss of friends and family due to religious prejudice, Mom and Dad were harassed because of their involvement with racially integrated groups. The neighbors accused my parents of bringing trouble into the neighborhood by inviting white people into our home. The white community saw the Faith only in terms of pro-integration, so they showed extra hostility toward us. Suddenly, our family was getting vicious telephone threats from who knows who, and we faced blatant social ostracism from both whites and blacks. To say that it was socially inconvenient would be a gross understatement. My mother sometimes said that joining the Bahá'í Faith was like committing "social suicide," but she continued to believe that "we have to do what we have to do." She and Dad refused to let all the animosities bother them, and went right on hosting Bahá'í gatherings at our home and advertising them in the newspaper. We lost friends, but we also gained new ones.

In the months that followed, my father lost contracts because of his Bahá'í involvement. But in the long run, the loss of business did not affect us economically. Dad had several acres of farmland that he worked on the side, so he spent more time growing and selling vegetables. Construction work that Dad lost would often come back to him when he would be called upon to redo the masonry or carpentry work that had been done badly by others. He was so good at his craft that he'd get calls to fix bad jobs, and then, of course, his contractors would have to pay him more. With time, the jobs picked up again. If there was a family financial crunch because of my father's initial loss of business, we kids never knew about it.

The hostility and ostracism that my parents and the various Greenville Bahá'ís experienced was not unique to Greenville. I never could understand it. The Bahá'í Faith is a multifaceted religion whose teachings include the oneness of God, the oneness of religion through progressive Revelation, the oneness of mankind, the equality of women and men, and the harmony of science and religion. The Faith offers practical guidance for mankind to establish peace in the heart, peace in the family, and peace on earth. And there is so much more. Bahá'u'lláh's teachings resolved every dilemma I have ever had concerning doctrines on topics such as Christ as the Son of God, the Trinity, Christ's Resurrection and Ascension, baptism, Satan, sin, heaven and hell, the limitless nature of the universe, and a long list of other topics. The Bahá'í Faith renewed my faith in Christ and transformed it into a broader perspective. It opened my heart, saved my life, and gave me hope for the future. But for most people who had never studied the Faith, when they looked at the Bahá'í community from the outside, all they saw was "different" and "integration." And both concepts scared them.

Taken by Surprise

My older brother Melvin had gone off to college years before and had since moved to Idaho and then San Francisco. I had always thought that Melvin was religiously inclined because he was the only person besides my mother and father who I can remember sitting in our living room reading the Bible. When I discovered the Bahá'í Faith in the fall of 1961, I wrote Melvin to tell him about Bahá'u'lláh, but he did not take my letters seriously. He later told me that he assumed I'd been taken in by a religious con man—a wolf in sheep's clothing. In a way, it was reasonable for him to assume that I didn't have any sense. During the years that I was drinking and delinquent, he'd hear all about my antics whenever he called home. He bemoaned my behavior saying, "Ricky is trying to find himself in the darkness." So when I wrote to him about the Faith, he automatically assumed that I was still stumbling around and that I had fallen for somebody's gimmick.

I later learned that when Melvin got my first letter about the Bahá'í Faith, he had phoned Mom to find out if she knew anything about this religion. I was not a part of that phone call, but years later Melvin told me what she said in response to his concerns. She told him, "Your Daddy and I thought that the Bahá'ís might be a bunch of communists, but Ricky has made so many good changes in his life! You know what he was like before. We had decided that the only thing we could do was to pray for him. But Melvin, you would not believe the person he is now. Ricky can't do enough for us! He's going to school every day, his grades have picked up, and he's so concerned about developing his character. Your Daddy and I had prayed for a change in Rick.

We didn't know our prayers would be answered in this way. So we decided not to forbid him to study this religion."

Meanwhile, I wrote Melvin several more letters which did nothing but fuel his concern.

In Spring of 1962, when my parents were actively investigating the Faith and hosting firesides, Melvin had some time in between jobs so he flew to Greenville to visit for several weeks. He took a taxi from the airport in order to surprise us. He arrived at our house about 9:00 at night to find the driveway and yard full of cars. He looked through the front window and saw many people—family members and others—sitting in the living room talking. He thought somebody must have died—that we were having a wake. He went around back of the house, came in through the porch door, and found Mom in the kitchen preparing refreshments. He asked, "Did somebody die? What are all these people doing here?" Mom said, "Nobody died. We're having a Bahá'í fireside." Melvin's jaw dropped in shock. He said, "Bahá'í? Aren't they communists?" My mother said, "No, Melvin, your Daddy and I were wrong. We started investigating this religion, too. We thought if it could do so much for Ricky, imagine what it could do for us!"

Melvin was dumbfounded as to how he could come home to find his parents studying a new religion. And he was especially confused as to how his little brother Ricky, the disgrace of the family, could be the ringleader. By that time, the informational part of the fireside was over, and Melvin mingled with our guests.

The next day, Melvin insisted on scheduling a special meeting with "this Eulalia Bobo lady" so that he could expose her as a fraud. The attendees at the meeting were Melvin, our friend Beau Miller, my sister Della, her husband Bobby, their friend Patricia Gamble, Mom and Dad, myself, and Eulalia. Now you've got to know that Melvin was smart, strong, and determined. He was an honor student, plus he went to college on a football scholarship. He was inducted into the Piedmont Athletic Association Hall of Fame. His football associates called him "the Bull." Nobody on the opposite team wanted to look up and see Melvin on the line because there could only be one outcome—you were goin' down. And Melvin was "on the line" when the meeting with Eulalia began. He knew the Bible and was ready to use it to prove that we had all lost our minds.

The Number 1 question of Melvin's was the Bahá'í understanding of the station of Jesus Christ. Did Bahá'ís believe, as Melvin did, that Jesus Christ was God? Eulalia said, "In a word, the answer is yes." Then she read from one of her books, quoting Bahá'u'lláh: "Were any of the all-embracing Manifestations of God to declare: 'I am God,' He, verily, speaketh the truth, and no doubt attacheth thereto. For it hath been repeatedly demonstrated that through their Revelation, their attributes and names, the Revelation of God, His names and His attributes, are made manifest in the world." She stopped there a minute to let that sink in, and then she continued in her reading, "And were any of them to voice the utterance, 'I am the Messenger of God,' He, also, speaketh the truth, the indubitable truth."[1]

We talked about that quote a long time. Eulalia used the analogy of the sun and sunbeams to describe the mystery of the relationship between the Manifestations of God and God. She explained that although our lives are dependent on the light, heat, and energy of the sun, we can't know the sun directly. But we can have direct contact with the sunbeams that bring the energy of the sun to earth in perfect measure to create and sustain life. Are the sunbeams the sun? From our point of view, yes, because they're our only access to the life-giving energy of the sun. But are the sunbeams literally the essence of the sun? No, and that's a good thing, because the full power of the sun on earth would be too much for humanity, and we'd all die.

Eulalia continued to explain that, similarly, the essence of the Creator is far too great to be known directly in the world of creation. But the Manifestations of God are like the sunbeams. They emanate the life-giving attributes of God to the world of creation, each in a perfect form that nurtures, inspires, and guides an ever-advancing civilization.

We talked some more, then Melvin excitedly pointed out that Bahá'u'lláh's teachings on the relationship between God, the Manifestation of God, and humanity solved a dilemma that he had struggled with for a long time. He turned to the Gospel of John in his Bible and read several verses he'd marked. One was "He that hath seen Me hath seen the Father."[2] "In these verses,"

Melvin said, "it's like God and Jesus are the same." Then he read a couple of other verses from the same Gospel: "I go unto to the Father: for My Father is greater than I"[3] and "No man hath seen God at any time, the only begotten Son . . . he hath declared him."[4] Melvin said, "Now in those two verses, there's a clear distinction between Jesus Christ and God." He said that he had wrestled with this distinction / no distinction problem for some time. But Eulalia's explanation made sense to him, so much so that he repeated it in his own words: "From one perspective, Jesus is God because He perfectly manifests the attributes of God. From another perspective, Jesus is the Messenger of God. The Messenger is necessary because the essence of God cannot be known directly by His creation. Both can be true at the same time depending on one's point of view."

Melvin was what they call a "quick study." In just a few hours, he was enthusiastically investigating the Bahá'í writings. He put forth all kinds of questions that he had never been able to resolve to his satisfaction in church—questions about baptism, heaven and hell, and topics in the Book of Revelation. He said, "This religion makes sense. I can accept these answers."

Melvin was especially impressed with Eulalia's knowledge and eloquence—so much so that he assumed she was a professor with a PhD at some outstanding university. He asked her about that, and she burst out laughing. She said, "Son, you've either got a vision problem or a hearing problem. I dropped out of school in the tenth grade. My brother Joe was always bailing me out of trouble. I was an alcoholic, always in and out of jail. That was my life. But I appreciate the compliment." She paused and then, with a smile, said, "I've gone from an alcoholic dropout to a PhD!"

That evening, after Mom and Dad went to sleep, the rest of us stayed up all night long talking with Eulalia. At eight o'clock in the morning, my mother invited us into the dining room to have breakfast, and we talked some more. At noon, Eulalia excused herself, saying, "I've got to go get some sleep. I just can't hang with you young people anymore!"

Eulalia was really a member of our family. We appreciated her warmth, knowledge, and example. I noticed that whenever she was scheduled to conduct a fireside at our home, she would first retreat to her room for a considerable amount of time—at least an hour. Once I asked her, "What do you do upstairs before the firesides? Are you studying about what you're going to say?" She said, "Oh, no. I go to pray. I go to pray that the right Eulalia comes down those stairs."

Detroit

By the time of Melvin's unexpected visit, my father's time had freed up quite a bit because he had lost a lot of work, including a major government building contract. He and Mom decided to make the most of this free time by taking a road trip to Detroit to tell her family about the Bahá'í Faith. Along with Melvin, my older sister, Della, was recruited to stay at our house to help take care of Phillip, Beverly, Sherry, Harold and me.

After Mom and Dad got on the road, they decided to take a detour to check on my older brother Charles Junior who was studying engineering at Tennessee State University in Nashville. They were not able to get in touch with Charles to alert him to their impromptu visit, nor did they have his address on them. So when they got to the campus, they just drove around asking people where Charles Abercrombie lived. Nobody seemed to know him. Finally, they asked a young man who said, "I don't think I know a Charles Abercrombie, but what does he look like?" When my parents described Charles the guy said, "Oh, you mean Partying Crump!"

This was unexpected. Charles had always been a lot like my father in that he tended to be serious-minded and hardworking. He took his responsibilities as the oldest child seriously and had been an excellent student. But apparently, Charles had discovered another side of himself in Nashville—one that liked to party down—and he had taken on "Partying Crump" as a nickname.

The guy led Mom and Dad to Charles' dorm where they found him immersed in his studies and they all had a good laugh over his new name. In the course of their visit, Mom and Dad discovered that, like themselves, Charles had been actively investigating the Bahá'í Faith. His interest came about like this: He had signed up for a class that was taught by Professor

Sarah Pereira* and was immediately impressed by her ability to connect with and inspire her students. When he learned that Dr. Pereira was a Bahá'í, the same religion that his little brother Ricky was so taken with, he began his own investigation of the Faith. He was surprised and pleased to learn of my parents' interest. Later that year, Charles joined the Bahá'í community. He went on to have a long career in the military, and in all of his travels he'd seek out the Bahá'ís of whatever country he was in. He got to know Bahá'ís all over the world.

After a short visit with Charles, my parents continued on to Detroit where Mom's mother, Della Mae Fowler Strange, lived along with Aunt Martha (Mom's sister) and other extended family members. We always called my Grandmother Della "Biggie," which is short for "Big Momma." Biggie was shocked to hear Mom and Dad talking about a new religion and she was not at all approving. The only person in our Michigan family who showed real interest in the Faith at that time was Aunt Martha's fourteen-year-old son, Bo Jack. This was partially because of a dream he'd had three years earlier. As a kid, Bo Jack didn't want to go to church. Then, when he was eleven, he dreamt that an elderly man with a beard told him, "The day will come when you won't have to go to church but, for now, you have to obey your parents." Bo Jack was strongly impacted by that dream and he did as he was told—he obeyed his parents and went to church without argument. When my father showed the family a picture of 'Abdu'l-Bahá, Bo Jack immediately recognized 'Abdu'l-Bahá as the elderly man in his dream.

My parents observed that Bo Jack easily understood the Bahá'í teachings and quickly took them to heart. He didn't get why Biggie was so resistant. He impatiently asked, "Biggie, don't you understand what Uncle Charles is saying?" Biggie retorted, "No! And you don't either!" Biggie frankly stated her opinion that Mom and Dad were crazy to be interested in a new religion. Nevertheless, Bo Jack followed his instincts, continued to investigate the

---

* For more information on the life of Dr. Pereira, see *Lights of the Spirit*, edited by Gwen Etter-Lewis and Richard Thomas.

Faith, joined the Bahá'í community that summer (with his parents' permission), and connected right away with the Bahá'ís in Detroit.

By the end of the week, my parents arrived back home. They were shocked to find Melvin, Harold, and Sherry in bandages. It was pure coincidence that during the week of their absence the three of them and a friend, Beau Miller, had ended up in the hospital emergency room. It could have happened at any time, really. The cause was a particularly rough football game that resulted in a couple of dislocated shoulders, a sprained ankle, and a fractured wrist. There were no permanent injuries.

After the Michigan trip, Dad continued to take every opportunity to teach the Faith, even though he had not yet signed a Bahá'í membership card. This activity worried a couple of the Greenville Bahá'ís who asked Hand of the Cause of God* Mr. Zikrulláh Khádem what they should do about Charles Abercrombie teaching the Faith without officially joining the Bahá'í community. Mr. Khádem advised that the response to my dad's teaching efforts should be nothing other than loving support and appreciation.

Memorized and Utilized

After a couple of weeks, Melvin pretty much recovered from his sprained ankle, and he and I had the great idea of going on a spiritual retreat camping trip in the mountains of North Carolina before he had to return to San Francisco. Our plan was to camp, float down the river, live off nature, and read Bahá'í books. Along with our camping supplies, we packed *The Hidden Words* and *Tablet of Aḥmad* by Bahá'u'lláh, plus 'Abdu'l-Bahá's *Some Answered Questions*. We also took *God Loves Laughter* and *Thief in the Night* by William Sears, and *Bahá'u'lláh and the New Era* by J. E. Esslemont. Our younger brother, Sherryfield—Sherry for short—was about eleven years old. Although he was not yet interested in investigating religion, he wanted to go

---

* The Hands of the Cause of God were made up of outstanding individuals—named by Bahá'u'lláh, 'Abdu'l-Bahá, and Shoghi Effendi—who were charged with protecting and propagating the Bahá'í Faith.

with us for the adventure and we were happy to have him. By then, he and I had recovered from the "Rat Teeth" incident. I have to tell you about that.

One evening, Sherry was in our backyard when he turned on the outside water faucet and started playing with water from the hose. He was getting all wet, and it was pretty cold outside. So, like a good older brother, I went to stop him. I was wearing a leather jacket, a long-sleeved sweater, and a long-sleeved shirt. As I took the hose from his hand, Sherry bit me on the arm through my leather jacket, through my sweater, and through my shirt. He broke my skin and drew blood out of my arm. He was "Rat Teeth" for a while after that. But by the time of this camping trip I was back to calling him "Sherry" again.

Our brother Harold drove Melvin, Sherry, and me to our camping site, about an hour's drive from home. Then Harold left with the plan that he would come back to the same spot to pick us up in five days. The three of us walked for some time until we were well into the woods near the river. As Melvin and I were setting up camp, Sherry walked down to the water to go fishing. On his way, he didn't notice the yellowjacket nest in a hole in the ground. He stepped on it, and the yellowjackets shot up his pants leg. At the campsite, Melvin and I heard hollering that sounded like some kind of screaming wildcat. But it was Sherry. When we saw him making his way back to camp, he looked like he was doing a new kind of dance, with elbows and knees going every which way. I called out, "How you doin' all that without music?" But then I saw them—yellowjackets coming out of his pants leg. Yellowjackets everywhere.

Melvin had chewing tobacco with him, so he tried to nurse Sherry back to health with tobacco juice—a folk remedy for stings—but to no avail. The three of us spent a sleepless, hot, and humid night battling mosquitoes and watching Sherry's right leg swell up and turn different colors. I used that long night to memorize Bahá'u'lláh's Tablet of Aḥmad, a special tablet for protection. As soon as the sun rose the next morning, we packed up with the intent of finding a store with a telephone so that we could call Harold to come and pick us up and get Sherry to a doctor.

Melvin's first idea was to build a raft and float down the river to the highway. We all agreed that would be the fastest way to get out of the woods and to a telephone. Melvin and I gathered several logs from fallen trees and wove them together with vines. The raft was big enough for the three of us and our gear, but it wouldn't float with all of us on it. It would only float with one person at a time. We'd wasted an hour and had nothing left to do but hike. I made Sherry a walking stick, and Melvin and I took turns half-carrying him since by that time his right leg had swollen up so bad he could hardly put weight on it. It was slow going.

In our cumbersome trek through the woods, we were moving along the top of a ravine among trees that held a lot of big woody hanging vines. They were probably frost grape vines, the kind that grow thick and run for hundreds of feet up and down trees and across the forest floor. We stopped to rest, and I noticed that Melvin was eyeing a substantial vine (probably three inches in diameter) hanging from a tree that was right on the edge of the ravine. He pulled hard on the vine and satisfied himself that it was well-attached to the top of the tree. He looked across the ravine, which was about twenty feet wide. Then Melvin followed the vine along the forest floor, pulled out his pocket knife, and cut the vine so that one end of it was free while the other was still attached to the top of the tree. The result was a length of vine on which he could, theoretically, swing back and forth from the tree and across the ravine. Now mind you, we did not have to cross the ravine to get to where we were going. It's just that Melvin decided he was going to show Sherry and me how to swing on a vine. Like Tarzan. Sherry and I sat back to rest and enjoy the entertainment.

Holding tight onto the vine, Melvin ran as fast as he could to get momentum and jumped off the edge of the ravine—seventy-pound backpack and all. It was right at the point where he kicked his legs up into the air to get onto the far bank when the vine broke, and Melvin tumbled down about thirty feet to the creek below. Luckily, it was a V-shaped gorge with sides of overgrown bushes, vines, and small trees. So he did more of a tumbling roll—not a nosedive to the bottom. He had a relatively soft landing. But the problem was that when he had cut the vine with his pocket knife, he cut it diagonally at a sharp angle, and as he was rolling and tumbling to the ground—still gripping the vine—he jabbed the sharp end of the vine right into his lower lip.

My amusement changed to concern as I watched Melvin's bravado turn into a dangerous accident. Melvin hollered up that he was OK. But now we had to get him out of there. I freed up another big vine and lowered it down so that he would have something sturdy to hold onto as he made the difficult climb up the side of the ravine. When Melvin finally got back to Sherry and me, his lower lip was bleeding and swollen. He looked like he had three lips.

There was nothing to do but carry on. Melvin and I continued to take turns supporting Sherry. After about an hour we made it to the highway, then followed the road until we came to a little country store. The storekeeper kept his distance. I don't know what he imagined, but we must have looked like something out of a horror movie. He let us use the telephone, anyway. We managed to call Harold, and he came to get us right away. When we were safely on our way back to Greenville and it was obvious that none of us were going to die, we relayed all of our unexpected adventures to Harold and suddenly everything became thigh-slapping hilarious. Harold could barely keep the car on the road for laughing.

Back in Greenville, Sherry and Melvin got the medical attention they needed and both of them healed up in short order. Ever since, whenever Melvin tells the story of that trip, he says, "It's a good thing that Ricky memorized the Tablet of Aḥmad that night, or we might not have made it out of the woods at all. On that camping trip, the Tablet of Aḥmad got memorized and utilized!"

Between You and God

After our camping trip, Melvin continued to study the Faith, and he joined the Bahá'í community that same year. Sherry declared himself a Bahá'í a few years later on his fifteenth birthday. Both Melvin and Sherry went on to serve the Faith in unexpected and adventurous ways.

In 1972, Melvin and his wife, Ida, moved their young family to Cherokee, North Carolina in order to teach the Faith and serve the people of the Cherokee Indian Reservation (also called the Qualla Boundary) in the Great Smoky Mountains. Melvin first worked on the construction of a state-of-the-art high school in Cherokee, then worked for the Bureau of Indian Affairs as an elementary school teacher and finally as a vocational rehabilitation counselor (helping those with disabilities get the assistance they needed to find a job). He also bought and ran a sawmill with one of his Cherokee friends. During the whole seven years that they lived in Cherokee, Melvin and his family lived in a log cabin with no electricity or running water. In every way you can imagine, they lived the life of a spiritual retreat in nature.

As for Sherry, in 2005, he moved to the Kingdom of Lesotho, a mountainous country encircled by South Africa, where he has been, to this day, establishing and operating Bahá'í schools that serve the greater community. Like Melvin, Sherry has had his own extended spiritual retreat in nature. Maybe our short-lived spiritual camping trip had a greater effect than we realized!

In early fall of 1962, Dad was ready to take his interview and officially join the Bahá'í community—that is, to become a voting member and also to be eligible to be elected to a position in Bahá'í administration. He asked me if he should wait until Mom was ready to officially declare as a Bahá'í, as well. I answered, "That is between you and God." A few weeks later, he decided to go ahead and establish his membership on his own. Fortunately, Greenville had its own Local Spiritual Assembly at that time, so he interviewed with the Greenville Assembly, demonstrated his deep knowledge of the Faith, and officially joined the community. My mother joined in the same manner some weeks later.

In addition to Mom, Dad, Melvin, and Sherry, all of my siblings joined the Bahá'í community. Della, Charles, and Harold joined in the fall of 1962, and Beverly and Phillip declared whenever they reached their fifteenth birthdays (the Bahá'í age of spiritual maturity).

- 8 -

The United Kingdom

Early in January of 1963, Virginia Ford (our Bahá'í friend who lived on Maco Terrace) asked me if I wanted to go to the Bahá'í World Congress in London. This gathering was to be the first of its kind—a huge event that would be held for the purpose of presenting to the Bahá'í world the first and newly elected Universal House of Justice, the supreme administrative body of the Bahá'í Faith. Thousands of Bahá'ís from all over the world would be attending. Virginia had made all the necessary preparations for the trip for herself, but for some reason she was not able to go, and she thought that I might want to go in her place.

The dates of Virginia's plane ticket extended about ten days past the Congress itself because she had also arranged to go on a guided tour of England. This entire prearranged package—the flight, the registration for the World Congress, the hotel reservation, and the tour—was available for me to purchase. Mom and Dad and I thought that this trip was a wonderful opportunity. It would necessitate my missing school for almost three weeks, but all of my teachers, as well as the principal of Sterling High School, gave me permission to be absent on the condition that I give reports about my trip when I returned. We discussed the finances, and it was agreed that I would go. I purchased Virginia's entire travel package, tour and all. Her itinerary was now my itinerary. I had just turned eighteen years old, I was a junior in high school, and not only would I be attending the first Bahá'í World Congress in London, but I'd be touring the United Kingdom as well!

When the time came, Martha Fettig, a Bahá'í who had recently moved to Greenville, drove me to New York City, where I caught the plane to London. Prior to this international flight, my only airplane ride had been in a lightweight four-seater plane piloted by my chemistry teacher, Mr. Peter A. Wittacker, who was a Tuskegee Airman (the first black aviators in the U.S. military who served so admirably in World War II). The ride in the four-seater had felt perilous. Whenever the wind blew, the direction of the plane changed. I'd be looking at some part of the landscape, and then, without changing my gaze, I'd be looking at something else.

But now I was over the Atlantic Ocean on a huge KLM (Dutch Airline) jet, and I felt like I was riding in a limousine. I immediately noticed that there were no black or white sections on the plane. I, as well as other African Americans, were seated among the white travelers. I thought, "This would never happen on the ground. Not in the South, anyway."

Although I was traveling by myself, I never once felt alone because there were a lot of Bahá'ís on the plane. Like myself, they were headed to London to attend the Bahá'í World Congress. One of them, Dwight Allen, a professor at Stanford, kept us entertained with card and magic tricks. The flight lasted several hours, and I remember it as a whole lot of fun.

Arriving in London, I took a taxi to the Royal Albert Hotel, where I had a room reserved. The Royal Albert Hotel was a high-end establishment, and one of its regular (no extra charge) guest services was to shine shoes and wash clothes. All I had to do was leave my shoes outside the door of my room when I went to bed at night, and they'd be shined by morning. Dirty clothes set outside the door would be cleaned and pressed overnight.

As I walked through the hotel, I saw that it was full of Bahá'ís from all over the world. Many were dressed in the traditional clothes of their countries, and all were sporting wide and welcoming smiles. I later learned that over seven thousand Bahá'ís attended that Congress and that they came from seventy countries. The Bahá'í communities in most places of the world at that time were very small, so to be in the presence of thousands of our coreligionists was a new experience for most of us. It was thrilling! For me, being under the same roof with all of these friends from every nationality was a powerful confirmation. Here we were, people of every color, from so many different religious and ethnic backgrounds, even speaking different languages, coming together in unity as Bahá'ís. I saw that unity in diversity could be a reality throughout the world.

From the hotel, we were able to take buses or taxis to Royal Albert Hall, the World Congress venue. Royal Albert Hall is a huge and impressive circular auditorium. Translation earphones were provided to all the attendees so that no matter what language was spoken on the stage, everyone in the audience could hear the speaker's message in his or her own language. Most of the talks were in English but not all, so my English earphones came in handy. Many of the talks were about the importance of 1963 as a holy year. The year was especially significant for three reasons: 1963 was the 100th anniversary of the Declaration of Bahá'u'lláh; it was the year of the election of the first Universal House of Justice; and it was the year of the first Bahá'í World Congress.

The election of the Universal House of Justice, which had taken place in Israel just days before, was a long-awaited event—a hundred years in the making! Although Bahá'u'lláh decreed the Administrative Order that required a Universal House of Justice, because its election required members of National Spiritual Assemblies* to serve as electors, the House of Justice could not be formed until there was a sufficient number of National Assemblies in the world to carry out that election. Many of the presentations focused on the history that led up to this great achievement.

I was most intrigued by the clear line of authority that shone like a golden thread through all of those years. From the time of the Declaration of Bahá'u'lláh in 1863 to His Ascension in 1892, the Bahá'í Faith had grown but had not achieved the worldwide capacity required to elect the House of Justice. After Bahá'u'lláh's Ascension, this growth continued under the guidance of two divinely appointed individuals—'Abdu'l-Bahá, and Shoghi Effendi. In His Will and Testament, Bahá'u'lláh named His eldest son, 'Abdu'l-Bahá (1844–1921), as the Center of the Covenant, meaning the One Who all

---

* A National Spiritual Assembly is the annually elected governing body of a national Bahá'í community.

Bahá'ís should turn to for authoritative guidance after Bahá'u'lláh's Ascension. In turn, in His Will and Testament, 'Abdu'l-Bahá named His grandson Shoghi Effendi (1897–1957) as the Guardian of the Bahá'í Faith, whom all Bahá'ís should look to for authoritative guidance after 'Abdu'l-Bahá's Ascension in 1921.

During his lifetime, Shoghi Effendi appointed thirty-two Hands of the Cause to serve as his deputies to protect and propagate the Faith. He referred to them as the "Chief Stewards of Bahá'u'lláh's embryonic World Commonwealth."[1] When Shoghi Effendi died in 1957, the Hands of the Cause guided the Bahá'í community until the election of the Universal House of Justice in 1963. And here is what I found most remarkable. When the Hands of the Cause called for the election of the House of Justice, they made themselves ineligible to be voted into that institution. I was amazed! The Hands of the Cause were the Chief Stewards of the Faith. One might think that such a position would tempt them to want to be elected to the Universal House of Justice, that they would be the likely candidates. But no, they removed themselves from the possibility of being elected to the Bahá'í' world's supreme governing institution. That purity of intent still touches my heart.

All of the newly elected House of Justice members were introduced at the Congress, and I was able to get personal signatures from most of them. There were also wonderful musical performances and other artistic presentations. I was surprised when a couple of the organizers asked me to speak at a small group session. My name was not officially on the program, but about an hour before a session started, I was asked to talk about how I learned about the Faith and also how all of my immediate family came to the Faith in such a short period of time. I don't remember exactly what I said, but I do remember the joy I felt as I shared my family's experience. Of all of the speakers and presentations, my heart was especially touched when Issam Tahan, an eight-year-old boy, chanted a Bahá'í prayer in Persian for his father, who was in prison in Morocco for the "crime" of declaring as a Bahá'í.

The entire Congress was like a dream, a paradise of unity in diversity. I made many friends, including John and David Chernesky who were near my age. We became close companions, looked out for each other, and usually sought out restaurants together. The three of us had our first experience with spicy Indian cuisine at an Indian restaurant in London. During my entire time in the United Kingdom, I never saw the racial prejudice that I experienced daily in the States. I encountered no separate seating for blacks in buses, had no problem getting seated in restaurants, and had no difficulty getting waited on in stores. At the Royal Albert Hotel, black people were treated with the same respect that the staff showed every other guest. It was amazing how quickly the equitable treatment felt normal to me.

You would think, with thousands of people coming together in one place from all over the world, that something might go wrong. But the Congress went smoothly for the whole five days. I know of only one related mishap. The Royal Albert Hall was close to Hyde Park, which is a beautiful recreational area that includes horse-riding trails. Linda Richter, a Bahá'í from the States, rented a horse to ride in the park. She had braces on her teeth that were to be removed shortly after returning home from the Congress. At one point, her horse ran under a tree limb. She couldn't duck fast enough, and she got whacked right in the mouth with the branch and sustained injuries that caused her to have to wear her braces for another year. That was the only accident I heard of. Linda healed up fine.

Touring

As a participant of the World Congress, I had the option of going on a guided bus tour of London, which included a stop at the resting place of Shoghi Effendi, the Guardian of the Bahá'í Faith. Of course, I signed up. When we arrived, I saw that the Guardian's gravesite was meticulously maintained as a beautiful, formal garden. To the side of the garden stood a small cottage that served as the caretaker's quarters, with one room that was a kind of museum and welcome center. Maps covered the interior walls of the museum room as well as photographs of Local and National Spiritual Assemblies—institutions that the Guardian had lovingly and painstakingly nurtured over many years. Shoghi Effendi had the largest and most beautiful gravesite in the whole cemetery. The flowers and everything were immaculate. I enjoyed meeting the caretaker, an extremely knowledgeable elderly gentleman. This trip was the first of three visits that I would make to the Guardian's resting place over the next fifty-four years.

When the Congress was over, I connected with the tour of the United Kingdom group that Virginia Ford had booked. There were about twenty of us from all over the world who were embarking on this weeklong trip. I was the only Bahá'í and the only African American, but we were all like family. During our travels, we stayed at hotels as well as guest houses (now they would be called bed and breakfasts). These were not hostel-style accommodations. We all had our own private rooms. During that week, we toured Wales; Stratford-upon-Avon, where Shakespeare was born; Bristol, which is famous for its universities; Stonehenge, an ancient monument that dates back as early as 3000 BC; the city of Bath, which had Roman baths built before the time of Christ; and Oxford, which is also famous for its universities.

When I got back to London after the weeklong tour, I realized that my funds had almost been depleted. I just hadn't brought enough money. This was problematic because I still had three days and three nights to go before my flight back to New York, and I also had to pay for transportation from New York to Greenville once I got back to the States. Looking back, I wish it had occurred to me to try to get in touch with the Bahá'ís in London, who I'm sure would have been happy to help me out with food and lodging. But I didn't think of that. Instead, I got myself a room at the most inexpensive rooming house I could find. Then I called my parents and arranged for them to wire me more money. It would be a day or two before the money would arrive.

The next day, I was concerned that I didn't have enough money to pay for both lodging and food before the additional money arrived. I figured food was more important than lodging, so I checked out of the rooming house. Later that evening, I found an all-night laundromat where I figured I could spend the night. I put my clothes in a dryer, and I went to sleep on one of the laundromat benches. About an hour later, a London Bobby (that's what the English call their police officers) came in and asked if those were my clothes in the dryer. I told him, "Yes." He informed me that the dryer had stopped, then he left. I sort of browsed around for five or ten minutes, then lay back down on the laundromat bench and went to back to sleep. After a short time, the same Bobby came back in, woke me up, and told me I was not allowed to sleep there. I had to pack up my clothes and leave.

After leaving the laundromat, I met a young man on the street and asked him, "Where is the cheapest place to stay in London?" He told me about a youth hostel in the London YMCA, so I went there. The price was $1.70 per night, including breakfast. That I could afford. I spent two nights at the YMCA. It wasn't particularly comfortable. I slept in a bunk bed in a big dormitory-type room with many other young men, but it was better than the laundromat. I got the wired money and was able to convert it to cash before my flight. I made it to the London airport, flew back to New York, and managed to return to Greenville healthy and fed.

New Notoriety

On returning to school, I gave reports of my time in the United Kingdom in every one of my classes. I showed photographs, programs, and brochures from the places I'd been. One of the outcomes of my new notoriety as a featured speaker was that my classmates began to see me in a new light. It was totally out of the box that anybody from Sterling High School would travel to Europe. It's true that some of my classmates' fathers had been to Europe while serving in the military. But a teenager, and a colored one at that, going to Europe by himself to attend a religious conference? To go on a weeklong sightseeing tour of the UK? In 1963? No, that was not normal.

But I had, indeed, traveled to the United Kingdom on my own and survived to tell about it. I had walked through Stonehenge, stood in its shadows, and felt its mystery. I had strolled around Shakespeare's birthplace and childhood neighborhood, Henley Street in Stratford-upon-Avon, Warwickshire. In the city of Bath, I had submerged my hands in waters from the same underground spring that had been a center of worship for the prehistoric Celts, later the stuff of healing legends, and the water source for an ancient Roman Bathhouse that was still standing. I had toured that bathhouse. Not only did I now know the difference between Romanesque and Gothic architecture, I had walked the grounds of Romanesque and Gothic-style buildings in Bristol, London, and Oxford. I had opinions on what buildings from the Middle Ages I thought were the most stunning, and I shared my opinions in my presentations.

But the greatest gift of that trip was that I was now standing in front of my entire class at Sterling High School, not only telling about the United Kingdom, but also sharing information about the Bahá'í Faith. My classmates and teachers were astounded that over seven thousand Bahá'ís from seventy different countries had gathered in London—they'd had no idea that this was a world religion. Teachers invited me to talk about the development of the Faith, its unique Administrative Order, and its principles. Previously, most of my classmates had disregarded the Bahá'í Faith as an obscure product of someone's imagination. But now they were seeing the Faith for what it was—a legitimate world religion. I was still sometimes the brunt of jokes whenever I tried to tell people about Bahá'u'lláh, but many more of my classmates began to take me and my Bahá'í interest seriously.

As news of my trip spread throughout school, it also spread through my extended family until it reached the ears of Biggie in Michigan. And she was not pleased.

- 9 -

Biggie

Shortly after I came back from London, Biggie, my maternal grandmother, made plans to come down from Detroit to stay with us and find out what was going on. She didn't like my parents' interest in the Faith, and the news that I had been to England on a Bahá'í trip worried her even more. Biggie had strong ideas about what we should and shouldn't be doing in the way of religion. My parents had, in her mind, corrupted her grandson Bo Jack the year before, and she was sure that we had all lost our minds and needed saving. The expectation of her arrival had all of us holding our breath.

Biggie was not a large woman. She was under five feet tall and probably weighed around one hundred and ten pounds most of her adult life. But despite her small stature, Biggie was the queen and the boss. My mother adored her. Every time my parents had a baby, Biggie came for three or four months to take care of Mom, the newborn, and the rest of us. Biggie was there for the birth of all eight of us. In fact, Mother simply would not have the baby until Biggie arrived. Biggie walked off just about every job she ever had to help Mother get back on her feet after childbirth. And whenever Biggie was in the house, she automatically became the head of the household. My father never interfered with Biggie, and that is saying something because you didn't just walk into my father's house and take over. But he relinquished his power to Biggie and let her be the boss.

My grandmother was an extraordinary woman in many ways. She was married to a man named Garfield Strange when she was a teenager, and had two daughters (my mom and Aunt Martha) before she was twenty. But when things turned out badly in the marriage, she divorced Garfield. And that was in the 1920s when women *didn't* divorce their husbands. Biggie felt that this separation was necessary because Garfield had a problem with jealousy, and the marriage had become physically dangerous for her. To protect herself and her daughters, Biggie left Garfield where he lived in Ware Shoals and moved forty miles north to stay with her parents in the outskirts of Greenville.

Early in their separation, Garfield asked Biggie's half-brother, Jack, to go get her and bring her back to Ware Shoals. Uncle Jack was big and tall, and spent a lot of time in Oklahoma working on ranches. He dressed like a cowboy—hat, boots, and all—all the time. Jack agreed to go get Biggie and bring her back to Garfield.

When Jack found Biggie, he tried to put her in his car against her will. He was strong enough to pick her up and put her wherever he wanted, but there was no way Biggie was getting in that car and going back to a life-threatening situation. So in the course of the struggle, Biggie started screaming "Rape!" as loud as she could. Now even though Jack was Biggie's half-brother, he had dark skin, and Biggie had light skin. She could pretty much pass for white. During this attempted kidnapping they were in an area where people didn't know either one of them. Jack knew, rightly enough, that this rape accusation could get him killed on the street, so he left Biggie alone and quickly drove off. Years later, under more peaceable conditions, Jack confronted Biggie about screaming like that in public. He said, "You could have gotten me killed!" She snapped back with, "Well, you were about to get me killed!"

Biggie loved her daughters, Lillie and Martha, and was absolutely devoted to them. At that time, the only work available to black women was being a maid or working in somebody's kitchen, so she worked as a domestic servant in Greenville. After the divorce, she and Garfield had a more cordial relationship, but he was absent as a father. He was not completely estranged from his daughters, but he didn't do much for them. For some reason, Dad made a point of staying in touch with Granddaddy Garfield. Granddaddy lived about an hour's drive from our house, and every once in a while, Dad would take us to visit him. Granddaddy would buy us candy whenever we came.

He'd take us to the corner store and tell the storekeeper to give us anything we wanted.

Sometime after I'd joined the Bahá'í community, we went to visit Granddaddy Garfield, and he offered to buy me a beer. I told him, "No thanks. I don't drink beer or anything like that. I'm a Bahá'í." He asked, "What's Bahá'í?" I explained to him that the Bahá'í Faith was a world religion founded by Bahá'u'lláh, and I told him about some Bahá'í principles and teachings. He said, "So, you done got the Holy Ghost? Let me see you climb that oak tree backwards." Then he started laughing. Granddaddy believed in Jesus, but he never would go to church because he felt that ministers were scoundrels. Over time, I had the opportunity to explain to him Bahá'í teachings about the appearance of the eternal Spirit of Christ throughout history—how the Word of God has guided humanity in progressive Revelation—and he liked that concept.

I got to know Granddaddy Garfield better when he was more advanced in age. He became disabled because of a stroke and needed some place to stay where people would take care of him. My mother and father invited him to live with us. He didn't want to stay at our home because he knew how he hadn't been a father to my mother when she was a child, and he was ashamed to accept our hospitality. But despite Granddaddy's objections, we took him in, and Mom, Dad, and the rest of us cared for him. He expressed a lot of unhappiness as an old man. Sometimes he'd just sit there and cry over what he had or hadn't done in his life.

One Way or Another

But back to Biggie's story. I believe it was in 1943 that Biggie moved to Detroit to work in a factory for the war effort (during World War II). Aunt Martha followed her up there. By that time, my mom and dad had been married for several years and had three children. But we still saw a lot of Biggie because, like I said, she'd come down to Greenville every time Mother had a baby. And when Mother was through having babies, Biggie still came to visit us almost every summer. The most fun grandmother ever, she was "on" all the time—keeping us doubled over in laughter at her hilarious comments, running after us, beating us in our own games of dirtball tag, and telling us stories that taught us the nobility of our heritage. It was always amazing to me how different my mother was from Biggie. Mother was soft-spoken and gentle with never an unkind word. Biggie, on the other hand, was rough and tough, with an outrageously colorful vocabulary. She had a heart of pure gold, and she was as assertive as gold is shiny. One particular occasion comes to mind.

It was the summer of 1957, shortly after the birth of Phillip, my youngest brother. Biggie was staying with us like she always did when mother had a baby. I was twelve years old, and it was the middle of summer. My older brother Harold and I had been given certain chores to do to help Biggie and Mom in the house. Melvin, however, who at the age of sixteen was already as big and robust as any man, was out working a construction job with my father. Midday, Dad and Melvin came home for lunch. When Melvin saw Harold and me washing dishes in the kitchen, he started teasing us, telling us that we were sissies, not men like him out on a job doing "real work." Biggie, who was also in the kitchen, told Melvin to leave Harold and I alone, go outside, and wait until lunch was ready. Melvin left the kitchen. But when Biggie stepped out to attend to laundry on the back porch, Melvin came back into the kitchen and continued to harass us about being sissies. Hearing him go on like that after she had told him to stop got Biggie worked up. She came barreling into the kitchen after Melvin. Melvin charged out of the kitchen running toward the front door. Biggie was right behind him. Harold and I were right behind Biggie.

When Melvin burst out of the front door and hit the porch, he went straight for the steps and cleared them in one giant leap to the ground. Then he turned right and headed for the driveway. His impressive jump had increased his lead. But when Biggie hit the porch, she immediately made a sharp right turn, took a few giant steps and jumped off of the right side of the porch. Melvin looked up and saw Biggie flying right at him. She landed squarely on top of Melvin and took both of them to the ground. They rolled down the paved driveway. Melvin started crying, then he started laughing, then he started crying again. Biggie was doing the same.

When they caught their breath, Biggie told Melvin, "Let this be a lesson to you. If I want you, I'm going to get you one way or another." And then she scolded him some more. Harold and I had the pleasure of watching the whole beautiful affair. Our grandmother had just decked our older brother with a flying tackle! My mother was horrified when Biggie came into the house with skinned knees and elbows. She told Biggie, "Those boys are getting too big for you to be tusslin' around with them." Biggie wasn't young-—she was in her early fifties at the time—but she was in good shape, and the incident didn't slow her down.

The point of the story is that *that* is how Biggie lived her life. She never let anything or anyone—friend, foe, or family—get the better of her, no matter what the situation was. Now here it was, 1963, and my parents and siblings and I were all in love with the Bahá'í Faith. I'd even been to Europe and back on a Bahá'í trip. Our new religious affiliation was contrary to Biggie's wishes, and she was coming down to Greenville to make things right.

I Thought You Were Dead

Upon Biggie's arrival, there was all the laughter and joyful greetings that we had come to expect with her visits. As she settled in, my parents, siblings, and I were enjoying the calm before what we expected to be a storm. But we had reinforcements—Eulalia Bobo was staying with us, and she would be our first line of defense. We were all looking forward to introducing Eulalia to Biggie. But when Eulalia first walked in to the kitchen to meet Biggie, they both froze. They just stood there staring at each other. We didn't know what to think. Then Biggie started to cry and said, "Child, I thought you were dead." Biggie and Eulalia embraced, and we all felt relieved and surprised. We came to find out that they had known each other in Detroit long before Eulalia had become a Bahá'í and during a time when Eulalia was struggling with some life-threatening situations. The two of them had lost contact over the years, and Eulalia had no idea that the "Biggie" we had talked about was the Della Mae Strange she had known years earlier. There was much celebration!

After a couple of days filled with catching up, Eulalia and Biggie started on the topic of religion. The fur flew. It was like the debates between my father and Eulalia all over again. Biggie insisted that Eulalia was wrong in her Bahá'í beliefs and that she was endangering all of our souls. Eulalia persisted in her appeals for Biggie to just consider listening to another way to understand and revere the Bible. Both of them were naturally loud and boisterous, and here they were wrestling with things that they were both passionate about. Mom and Dad gave them space and just let them go at it.

Mostly I kept out of the way. But after just a few days, things quieted down, and I'm happy to share that I was in the room when a new light came on in Biggie's eyes. Her major point of contention had been that all of the Bible—the Old Testament and the New Testament—had to be taken at face value and anything other than a literal interpretation was an abomination that would put Eulalia and all of us in the fires of hell. Biggie's turning point came when, through Eulalia's patient teaching, she realized that those who interpreted the Old Testament prophecies literally—the Pharisees and others mentioned in the Gospels—failed to recognize Jesus Christ as the promised Messiah. This was like a crack in a wall that let the light in. For several days, the two of them studied Messianic prophecies in the Hebrew scriptures and looked for the nature of the fulfillment of those prophecies in the New Testament. Were they fulfilled in a literal material manner, or were they fulfilled in a spiritual way?

I joined Eulalia and Biggie in their study whenever I could and I learned a lot. For example, I learned that the Old Testament Book of Isaiah prophesies that the Messiah would sit on the throne of David and conquer the East and the West.[1] The expectation at the time of Christ was that the Messiah would gain an earthly throne and wield military and political power, like a king. But Christ never had an earthly throne. And he didn't physically conquer so much as a village. Clearly, that prophecy was not fulfilled in a material way. But, according to Bahá'í teachings, that prophecy was fulfilled in a spiritual manner. Christ, the Word of God, occupied the spiritual throne of David in the heaven of divine will, and He conquered the kingdom of hearts in the East and the West by the sword of His utterance.[2]

I also learned that the Book of Isaiah prophesies that the Messiah would magnify Mosaic Law.[3] A popular interpretation of this prophecy was that the Messiah would strengthen, spread, and enforce all of the ancient laws attributed to Moses. But Christ not only failed to magnify these laws in this literal sense, but He actually broke some of them, including the law of the Sabbath. However, the Bahá'í writings explain that Christ did fulfill this prophecy in a spiritual sense. Every Manifestation of God confirms the foundational truths of the previous Revelation and magnifies them—that is, gives these truths higher expression—in new teachings and social laws suited to the era in which He appears.[4]

It became clear to Biggie that insistence on literal interpretation of these and other prophecies had resulted in many denying Christ as the Messiah. Consequently, she became amenable to looking at spiritual interpretations of biblical scripture found in the teachings of Bahá'u'lláh. Gradually, Biggie came to recognize Bahá'u'lláh as the Manifestation of God for today. She embraced the Bahá'í teachings as the Word of God, and her appreciation of Eulalia's enthusiastic and patient teaching was boundless. Biggie especially delighted in the realization that she could claim the entire history of the Cause of God—from before Krishna and including Abraham, Moses, Buddha, Zoroaster, Jesus Christ, Muhammad and Bahá'u'lláh—as her spiritual heritage.

The impact of Bahá'u'lláh's writings on Biggie's heart was undeniable. She had always preached that blacks and whites were equal, but the Bahá'í Faith gave her a new perspective that went much deeper than what she had originally thought. She had been all about Black Power, Louis Farrakhan, and Black Nationalism. She had promoted the idea of separate but equal—that blacks should have their own businesses, their own neighborhoods, their own police forces, their own cities, and their own countries. And if this separation had to be achieved through violent means, then so be it. Through Bahá'u'lláh, Biggie came to understand that separate but equal is not the answer. Every community needs to have equality with unity, and this can be achieved through the realization of the oneness of humanity, consultation, study of the sacred text, and service.

During her visit, Biggie met all of the Bahá'ís in upstate South Carolina and quite a few visitors from other areas. My grandmother enjoyed all the Bahá'ís, but she seemed to have special feelings for Junie Faily. A lot of people wouldn't get into a car that Junie was driving because once Junie started talking, she'd turn her head to look at the passengers, and she might not look at the road for a minute or two. Or three. But Biggie would willingly ride with Junie. Biggie told us, "Junie don't be driving that car. Bahá'u'lláh's driving that car. I'd rather be in a car that Bahá'u'lláh's driving than you people."

Although the Bahá'í Faith redirected her life in a good way, my grandmother always kept her fiery disposition and unexpected sense of humor. When Biggie was in her nineties, my sister Beverly told her that perhaps she needed to be a little gentler in her speech because Bahá'u'lláh taught that words can cut like a razor. Biggie shook her head and quipped, "Bahá'u'lláh don't know the people I know." On her 101st birthday she said, "If I knew I was going to live to be a hundred and one, I'd have taken better care of myself."

She lived to be a hundred and two.

- 10 -

Wheels

By my junior year in high school, a lot of my friends depended on me for transportation because I had a car—sometimes, two cars. That was not because my parents bought me cars, but because, well, frankly, I could fix anything. My friends and I would find car parts from junk lots and various other places, and I'd use them to get the most unlikely vehicles on the road.

My first automobile was a light green 1949 Pontiac Straight-8. That car was almost as old as I was. I paid $25.00 for the car, then had to pay $35.00 for a new battery! I worked on it and drove it for a while, then traded it in for a 1956 turquoise Oldsmobile V-8. That car had a powerful engine. It sounded like an army tank. During the time I had the Oldsmobile, I also owned a green 1934 Ford Coupe which I'd resurrected from a junk yard. It could seat a driver and one passenger in the front, and it also had a rumble seat in the back big enough for two. That Coupe was my pride and joy.

Because I had my own car, I was often asked, "Rick, how about a ride to the football game?" "Hey, Rick. How about a ride to the party?" or "Hey Ricky, what about a ride to the movies?" I was my friends' wheels. I enjoyed the parties, movies, and games, but my greatest interest—where I found the most joy, and what I most wanted to share with my friends—was Bahá'í firesides. So after a while, when my friends would ask me for a ride, I started saying, "Sure, I'll take you, but then you've got to go to a fireside with me." My friends dodged me on this for a time, but when I started dodging their ride requests as well, a few of them finally responded with, "OK, I'll go to a fireside with you." One of these friends was William (Smitty) Smith.

It was the spring of 1963, and Smitty had reluctantly agreed to go to his first fireside. I had promised to drive the '34 Ford Coupe, and Smitty was looking forward to riding in it. Smitty got in the front seat, and a couple other friends climbed into the rumble seat in the back. That evening, the fireside was at the Bensons' house. When I turned into the Overbrook Circle area, Smitty and the others objected loudly and almost bailed out because they thought I was going to get them all killed. They knew, rightly enough, that it was perilous for black kids to go into white neighborhoods, especially at night. If we weren't carrying a work shovel, a hoe, or showing some other sign that we were there because we were hired help, it was dangerous—very dangerous. I tried to assure them, "No, it's all right, it's all right." As I parked in the Bensons' front yard, Dick came out calling, "Is that you, Ricky?"

My friends were struggling with their dilemma: whether or not to get out of my car. They figured that if they went into a white person's house, there'd be big trouble. That was not a step they were willing to take. But they also thought that if they stayed outside and the neighbors saw them, there'd be bigger trouble. So they came in. Like myself at my first fireside, for the first time in their lives, they were in an integrated social setting. There were about twenty people in the living room. Right away, Smitty spotted Ms. Annie Herd, one of his grandmother's best friends from Springfield Baptist Church. He figured that if Ms. Herd was there it must be okay, so he relaxed some. Then he recognized Junie Faily, the "white lady."

You will recall that Junie had met Helen Strawder (the birthday party Helen) at Springfield Baptist Church. Well, that's the church that Smitty's family went to, and he remembered seeing Junie there. Apparently, Junie had been going as a visitor to Springfield Baptist on the first Sunday of every month for years. And each time, when asked to introduce herself along with the other visitors prior to the service, Junie would stand up and say, "I'm Junie Faily. I'm a Bahá'í. We believe in the oneness of the human family, and I've come to worship with you today." And then she'd sit down. She was regular as clockwork with these visits, so much so that the kids came to look forward to her visiting day. They called it "white lady Sunday." But Junie didn't just visit the church. She also invited the women from the church to her home for tea. Now this was absolutely unheard of. The women at Smitty's church were totally taken by the fact that this little white woman would invite them to her home. That led to some of the women coming to the Bensons' firesides, so there sat Ms. Herd.

That meeting inspired Smitty and the other friends to want to learn more about the Faith, so they started asking me for rides to firesides. Smitty was struck by the fact that the Bensons and the Abercrombies alternated fire-sides—white neighborhood, then black neighborhood—with the same group of integrated people. The blacks went to the whites' homes, and the whites went to the blacks' homes. It was not just a one-way thing. Smitty saw the equality and a depth of relationship that our Bahá'í community manifested, and this was one of the factors that fueled his enthusiastic investigation of the Faith.

"What Are You Doing About That?"

With my new notoriety as a world traveler, and with the Bahá'í Faith established as a legitimate religion worthy of classroom attention, more of my friends at Sterling High School became interested in the Faith. By the summer of 1963, many of my classmates had declared as Bahá'ís. When I was first introduced to the Faith, the Greenville Bahá'í community consisted of just a handful of adults, not even enough to form a Local Spiritual Assembly. But with all these youth declarations, suddenly there were more teenagers in the Greenville Bahá'í community than adults—and all of them were black. They brought a special energy to our community meetings and firesides. We had quite a few musicians, such as Charles Hall, who played a lively piano. We would sing Bahá'í songs and black spirituals, sometimes until two or three in the morning. With the influx of young people, our Bahá'í firesides became even more exciting with more energy, new questions, and different perspectives.

This influx of black teenagers into the Bahá'í community was a cause for celebration, but it also presented rich learning opportunities. One example that comes to mind involved Grace von der Heydt. Grace was a proper and sophisticated white businesswoman who had been raised in New England high society. She was an aristocrat. She spoke in support of Bahá'í principles, including race unity, but her manner to the new black declarants did not appear friendly. It seemed evident that Grace resisted giving rides to black teenagers who needed transportation to Bahá'í events. All of us teenagers noticed, and because we were not yet fully aware of the Bahá'í prohibition against backbiting, we inappropriately discussed our opinions about Grace among ourselves. In the course of our discussion, somebody dared one of the new teenage declarants, Curtis Butler, to publicly confront Grace about what we saw as her prejudicial attitudes.

Not too long after that, when Grace, other adults, and several of the youth were gathered around our dining room table, Curtis openly told Grace that the youth had been discussing her behavior and believed that she was prejudiced against black people. You'd have to have seen her face. She was clearly taken aback. All of us froze. For a long while, there was silence as Grace just studied Curtis. Finally, she said to him, "Yes, I am prejudiced. But I am also trying to do something about it. Now, because you have confronted me here, in this manner, I believe that you are stupid. What are *you* doing about *that*?"

Curtis had to laugh. We all did. Grace's forthright honesty changed the way the youth thought about her. It was a breakthrough for everybody. From that day on, the youth had no problem with Grace, and in turn, she continued to work through her admitted prejudice. She even offered rides. One time, Grace told my father, "Charles, you know, you've never hugged me." My father said, "Grace, I never thought you wanted to be hugged by me." She said, "Well, you were wrong." And they hugged each other.

The beautiful thing about Grace is that even though she struggled with feelings of bigotry, she didn't stay away from black people, and she intentionally worked on herself in this regard. When she went on her Bahá'í pilgrimage, she openly shared that one of her intentions during pilgrimage was to pray for assistance in detaching herself from her inherited prejudices. Grace was a wonderful role model for all of us.

Crossing the Line

The Bahá'í youth in Greenville were close friends. We all went to Sterling High School. We socialized a lot and we also traveled around South Carolina, North Carolina, and Georgia to speak at firesides and participate in Bahá'í activities. The fact that we were all African American made traveling around relatively safe because, in any combination of girls and boys, we were an all-black group. We knew the written and unwritten rules of segregation in the South and what lines not to cross. But there was no way to not cross those lines when white Bahá'í youth came to join us.

It was the summer of 1963, and several Bahá'í teenagers from other areas—black and white friends whom we had met at Penn Center and other venues—spent several weeks in Greenville to help us with our Bahá'í teaching work. Many of these visiting youth stayed at our house. My cousin Bo Jack was with us for the summer, too. Bo Jack was as much family to me as my biological brothers and sisters. Although he had been born and raised in Detroit, ever since he was a child Bo Jack had spent summers with our family. In fact, he was with us so much that some of our friends assumed he was an Abercrombie.

As a group, we all got along great and had a lot of fun. Patsy Sims, a white Bahá'í, was one of these summer service visitors. Patsy was from Tennessee, and she had a down-home country manner about her. Bo Jack, Patsy, and I had just left Virginia Ford's house on Maco Terrace (where Patsy was staying) and were walking down Ackley Road on our way to my house when Patsy decided that she wanted a piggyback ride. She jumped onto Bo Jack's back. Well, Bo Jack took off running down the street with Patsy on his back and her hollering and making a lot of noise—all in fun.

Until a police car pulled up. A black guy running down the street with a screaming white girl on his back? It could have turned out badly for Bo Jack. But we explained to the policemen that we were with a Bahá'í group and headed to the Abercrombie home. The police were plenty familiar with the Bahá'í gatherings at the Abercrombie's, and once it was evident that we were all "part of them Bahá'ís," Bo Jack was not arrested for kidnapping a white girl.

One day, six of us made a day trip to North Carolina for a teaching event. We were an integrated group of girls and boys that included Nolan Babb (one of my classmates from Sterling High School), Patsy Sims, and a few others. I was driving my Oldsmobile because it would seat six or seven people easily. But that evening, as we were on our way back to Greenville, the car's battery holder broke and hit the fan, which drove a piece of the battery holder into the radiator causing a bad leak.

We were losing water fast. I stopped at a gas station and asked if I could get water for the radiator. The white attendant looked at the mixed company in the car, shook his head, and said, "No. We don't have any water." Meanwhile, three other white men came out of the gas station, took a look at us, and started walking toward my car. I could see their hostility, so I jumped into the driver's seat and drove off as fast as I could. As I pulled away, I could see in my rearview mirror that the three of them had gotten into a pickup truck and had taken off behind us. I drove fast enough to stay ahead of them, and luckily—while just out of their sight due to a curve in the road—I took a sharp right off the highway onto the Blacksburg exit. They didn't know I'd made that turn, and they continued on the highway. After a few seconds, we saw them go on up across the overpass.

We laid low for a little bit, then got on the highway again. I stopped at the next gas station and asked about water as well as the possibility of getting the radiator fixed. While I had the hood of my car up, this big white man—I don't know if he worked at the gas station or not—approached the car with a screwdriver, like he was going to help fix the leak. I stepped back to give him some room. But instead of trying to fix the problem, he started punching holes in the radiator with the screwdriver! I grabbed his arm to make him stop, but then he grabbed a hold of a spark plug wire which caused me to get shocked. In that kind of electrical situation, it's the person at the end that gets the worst shock. Just then Nolan came up behind him, grabbed the man by the shoulders, picked him up, and slung him down to the side. Nolan was big, and he knew how to use his strength. I slammed the hood down, we jumped into the car, and took off.

Now the radiator was leaking worse, so we stopped at yet a third gas station. Here there was no hostility and, happily for us, the white attendant told me how to do a temporary repair. The procedure was to get some red mud from a bank at the side of the road, stuff the radiator holes with the mud, run the engine so that the fan would dry the mud to a hard clay, then add water to the radiator. He said the quick fix should get us to Greenville but that I should replace the radiator as soon as possible. The idea made sense, and I commenced with the repair, doing exactly as he instructed. I also used the gas station public phone to call one of my estranged cousins from Spartanburg, John Clifton Abercrombie Junior. I asked him to come and transport the girls who were with us. My concern was to get the girls back to Greenville in a car that wasn't going to break down. Although we hadn't seen each other for a year or so (because of his father's disapproval of the Faith), John Clifton graciously met us at the gas station and got the girls back to Greenville safely. I finished the repairs and drove the rest of us home without any further incident. Over a week went by before I got a new radiator. But I have to tell you that during that week, the mud-repaired radiator never leaked a bit. Not one drop.

At the first two gas stations, we were treated badly not because we were a Bahá'í group—those people didn't know what religion we were. Rather, they were hostile because we were a racially integrated group. For us Bahá'í youth, there were many such incidences and near-getaways while traveling here and there in our integrated fashion. Our purpose was not to cause an uproar. We were just doing what we needed to do in order to be authentically who we were.

- 11 -

Open Doors

It was sometime during spring break, 1964. My alarm went off early as was typical on Saturdays when I had yardwork to do. I groggily got out of bed, stepped into the hallway, and tripped over a body. It was a guy in a sleeping bag. I should've been more careful. My parents had an open-door policy. It was not unusual for Bahá'ís to come to our house needing a place to stay, and they were always welcome. That particular summer morning, a dozen or so youth I'd never seen before had come to our house in the middle of the night and were sleeping all over the place. Over the past year, our house had become not only a center of Bahá'í activity in Greenville, but also a haven for Bahá'ís traveling in the southeast. My brother Charles, who was usually away at school, came home one evening to find a dining room full of strangers wondering who *he* was. He laughingly told me, "I had to explain myself to get a seat at the table!"

Our house was unusually big, especially for a black family at that time. It had two stories, eight bedrooms, two full baths, a formal living room, formal dining room, family room, large eat-in kitchen, long back and front porches, and a large basement on a quarter-acre plot of land. My parents bought the house in 1945 when they had only four children. When they were looking to buy a house, they weren't sure that they needed one that was so big, but they both fell in love with it. I was the first baby to be brought home to 8 Rebecca Street, and then there were three more babies—eight children altogether. We could have lived in a house a fraction of the size, but the bounty of an extra big home became evident as my mother and father began hosting events

111

as well as a regular stream of travelers. My mother said, "Bahá'u'lláh was guiding our steps long before we knew it!"

Behind the Magic

Not only was our home welcoming in terms of size, but the food was bountiful and delicious. My mother was a genius in the kitchen. Guests would comment on how multiple-course meals seemed to appear like magic on our table. I'd like to dispel the "magic" myth here and share a little bit about how this hospitality happened. In truth, it was a combination of horticultural skills, animal husbandry, brilliant time management, organized inventory, creative food processing, serious culinary skills, and human resource management that went on all year long in the context of my parents' loving relationship.

We had a garden in our backyard that my mother kept, and we also had twenty-something acres of land in the southern part of Greenville County that my father worked on weekends and after his regular construction jobs. We called it the big garden, but some would call it a farm. Our neighbors by that land were Mr. Cureton, Dad's brother Marion, and Mr. Bannon. Daddy plowed the land every season with Mr. Cureton's tractor, then he would borrow Uncle Marion's mules for the planting and the plowing that had to be done during growing season. I had an especially memorable experience with one of those mules.

I was fourteen years old. It was early summer when Daddy and I went out to our acreage in the morning. He borrowed a mule from Uncle Marion, harnessed the mule, and got it hooked up to a plow. We had an acre or so of corn, and my task was to lead the mule to plow between the planted rows. This plowing aerates the soil, gets rid of weeds, and also throws dirt over the roots which serves as fertilizer and mulch for the corn. My father had to go to a construction site, but he said he would be back around noon with my lunch. This was during the time when I thought I knew more than, well, anybody. Our neighbor Mr. Bannon had a manmade lake on his property, and I figured that if I finished my plowing job fast enough, I could go swimming in Bannon's lake. So as soon as my father drove off, I did exactly what I knew I shouldn't do. I started running the mule up and down the rows of corn.

Now anybody who knows farming knows that you don't run a mule. Mules are made for endurance, not for speed. But I wanted to get into that lake before lunchtime, so that mule and I were flying. Meanwhile, my father realized that he had forgotten something, so he turned his truck around and came back to the corn field. I was running up a row in the opposite direction, so I didn't see him until I started running back down. When I reached Dad, he quietly said, "Give me the mule." He unhooked the mule from the plow, took off the harness, and returned the mule to Uncle Marion. Then he came back to me, handed me a hoe, and said, "Finish the plowing." I hoed that field all day long and into the evening. Never made it to Bannon's lake. That was the last time I ever ran a mule.

We grew a lot of vegetables, and of course all this produce had to be processed. Mother did some canning in our kitchen, but mostly we canned at the government cannery in Greenville. People don't use canneries much anymore, so let me tell you about that. First, we'd clean and chop the vegetables in our kitchen. Then we'd take the prepared produce to the cannery and put it into sterilized cans. A narrow conveyer belt moved the cans to two or three cannery workers who operated the machines that stamped the lids of the cans on, one can at a time. Those workers put the sealed cans into a big wire basket and lowered it into a pressure cooker. The cans stayed in the cooker about an hour, then were lifted out and lowered into a cooling pond. The water in the cooling pond was always a little bit warm. We never actually got into the cooling pond, but when we were little, we'd play along the side of it.

Canning was a family project for us. Mom, Dad, and usually four or five Abercrombie kids would be at the cannery to do the work. If other people were ahead of us, we would help them in order to get things moving faster. And while we were waiting for our cans to cook and cool, we'd help those who came behind. It got to where people would call the cannery to ask whether or not the Abercrombies were there. If we were there, they'd show up. If not, they'd put off canning until we were there to help. We canned our food and half the neighborhood's.

Canning was not a once-a-year event, but something that we did often in the spring, summer, and fall growing seasons. In addition to the vegetables we grew, we'd buy massive amounts of fruit in season and make, for instance, applesauce and fruit preserves. One year we processed over five hundred cans of peaches. It didn't happen often, but occasionally the seal on a can would fail, the food inside would spoil, and we'd hear the can explode in the basement pantry. Bang! I can tell you that spoiled lima beans smell the worst.

My parents raised their own pork on their land, too. The pigpen went down to the creek, so the pigs always had water. In order to make slop to feed the pigs, we'd get leftover food that would otherwise be thrown away from the cafeteria of J. L. Mann High School. My father would put it in a fifty-five-gallon drum and cook it over a big fire, then he'd feed it to the pigs. He also grew corn as pig feed. When we'd slaughter a hog, we'd make lard and pork rinds (cracklings) out in the back yard in a big three-legged cast iron pot over a fire. For a while, my parents kept chickens in our back yard, and also a cow or two. But when our neighborhood was annexed into the city, the ordinances changed to where we couldn't keep livestock in our yard anymore.

When you grow and process your own food, there is work to do pretty much all the time—not to mention the many other chores involved in maintaining a household of ten people. That's where Mother's management skills came in. She was the first equal opportunity employer I'd ever known. There were eight Abercrombie children, and at any point in time, all of us had our age-appropriate tasks related to food processing and other household tasks. Mother was the Chief Operations Officer of the Abercrombie household, and she carried out that job magnificently. And even though her hands were constantly busy, she always had time for others. You might come to her for a listening ear and she would give you one hundred percent of her attention and the best advice you ever heard. You wouldn't even notice that the whole time she was shelling peas, snapping beans, or making peach cobbler.

Putting a multiple-course meal on the table for two dozen or so people seemed effortless for Mom. She'd reach in the freezer and get out however much meat she needed, send one of us down to the basement to get canned vegetables, and send another one of us to the backyard garden to get fresh greens. While the meat cooked (my mother had her own technique for quickly cooking frozen meat) she and whoever she chose as her assistant would heat up two or three pots of different kinds of vegetables, cook a pot of rice, and make some biscuits and gravy. Then she'd pull out a sweet potato casserole and pies she had made that morning, and a big dinner for a house full of people would be ready in under forty-five minutes.

The most welcoming and gracious hostess on the planet, my mother's greatest joy was bringing people together in service to the Faith. One day, I asked her what she wanted to be remembered for. She said, "I want to be remembered for my love for my fellow man." My mother showed that love. And her service to the Bahá'í Faith was, in a large part, to serve the friends who came into her home. Although she did not travel for the Faith as my father did, she did not need to. The world came to her.

My sister Beverly has traveled to forty-eight states and to many foreign countries in her service to the Faith, and wherever she has gone, there has always been someone who greeted her with joy and shared remembrances of time spent at the Abercrombie home. Beverly served at the Bahá'í World Center from 1997 to 2002, where she would see Bahá'í pilgrims from all over the world, and often in a pilgrim group, someone would approach her saying, "Oh Beverly, I had the best coffee and biscuits I've ever had in your mother's kitchen!"

Portal to the World

My parents' welcoming spirit turned our home into a kind of portal to the world as Bahá'ís from all over the United States, and many from other parts of the planet, would come and stay with us. More than once, we hosted Persian Bahá'í families just arriving into the United States as immigrants. All of these visitors helped our teaching work and encouraged our local community. They also helped us learn about places we'd never been. Mrs. Jalali, a Persian Bahá'í who lived in North Carolina, would often stay with us for a few days to help my mother host regional Bahá'í meetings or other special events. Sometimes Mrs. Jalali would make delicious Persian food in our kitchen. My mother's favorite was *Lubia Polo,* a dish made with rice, tomatoes, green beans, and Persian spices.

I had met Mrs. Jalali's son, Fereydoun Jalali, at Penn Center at the regional Bahá'í summer school of 1962. We had had a lot of fun together. Fereydoun was a vegetarian—the first vegetarian I'd ever met. Sometime later that year, Fereydoun came to our house for a meeting of the Southeastern Bahá'í School Committee. My mother had made dinner for everybody, and it included fried chicken. Now Mom's fried chicken was something that nobody could refuse, including Fereydoun. That was the end of his vegetarian diet, at least when he was in Greenville. Whenever Fereydoun came to our house, he'd be hoping for fried chicken and he was never disappointed.

Another one of our many memorable visitors was Matthew Bullock (1881–1972), an older African-American gentleman who had been a successful attorney. He was invited to come to Greenville to give some Bahá'í talks, and he took my parents up on their invitation for him to stay at our house for a couple of nights. As it worked out, we talked him into staying with us for about a month.

Matthew had lived an incredibly rich life. He had been a talented athlete, a winning football coach, a war hero, a civic leader, an accomplished singer, a church leader, and a Harvard Law School graduate. He also had an intriguing story of how he became a Bahá'í. He had known of the Faith since early adulthood, and in fact, had known Louis G. Gregory (1874–1951), one of the earliest Bahá'ís in the United States and also a black attorney. For years, Matthew associated with Bahá'ís, but he did not feel moved to study the Faith. Later in his life, a Bahá'í friend, Ludmilla Von Sombek, handed him a Bahá'í book and said, "I have to give a talk on the Faith, and you could help me by reading this book and underlining what you see as the highlights." Matthew consented. After a few weeks, he brought the book back to Ludmilla. He had underlined every word.

Matthew wholeheartedly accepted Bahá'u'lláh's teachings and became a member of the Bahá'í community in 1940. Although he was in his sixties when he came to the Faith, Matthew's Bahá'í service included assisting Bahá'í communities in the Caribbean, Belgian Congo, and Liberia, and serving on the National Spiritual Assembly of the Bahá'ís of the United States. He told us of the places he'd seen and the fascinating people he'd met. Our worldview grew with each story.

Matthew was, without a doubt, the most dignified and proper gentleman I've ever met. He wore a suit and tie *every single day*. He's the only man I've ever seen eat a hamburger with a knife and fork. My younger brother Phillip, who was about seven years old at the time when Matthew was staying with us, was completely enamored of "Mr. Bullock" and asked him, "Will you be my grandfather?" Matthew answered, "Yes, Phillip, I will be your grandfather."

Jack McCants was another frequent visitor and dear friend of the family who enlarged our view of the world. Jack was particularly well-schooled in the Christian tradition because he had originally been a minister of a Methodist church in Texas. I was amazed by his story. When Jack was a preacher, things were going well for him and his church. But then it happened that serious labor issues arose in a local manufacturing plant. About half of his church members went on strike, while the other half crossed the picket line. This split on the labor issue caused bitter antagonism that was tearing the church apart. During this difficult time, Jack happened to visit a black church, and he was especially moved by the choir. He thought that the spirit of the choir could really help his parishioners, so he invited the black choir to come to sing at the white church he served. This was in 1954.

The choir came and sang, but the churchgoers gave the choir a cold reception and Jack was reprimanded by the deacons: "What do you mean, bringing those colored people into our church?" Things were a mess and Jack's heart was broken. He left that church and decided to take a break from being a minister. Jack didn't give up his ordination, but he chose not to have another church assigned to him right away. Shortly after he gave up his church assignment, he was drafted into the U.S. Army.

Jack heard about the Bahá'í Faith for the first time when he was going through basic training at Ft. Sam Houston in Texas. A fellow trainee, Stephen Suhm, gave him a copy of John Esslemont's classic introduction to the Bahá'í Faith, *Bahá'u'lláh and the New Era*. But Jack didn't pursue its study because he was soon sent to serve in South Korea. He got there just as the Korean War had ended and was assigned to a medical company of a U.S. Army Division located on the South Korean side of the Demilitarized Zone (DMZ).

Even though the war was over, the violence continued. North Koreans soldiers often got through the concertina wire of the DMZ at night and killed soldiers and civilians in South Korea. Living in the postwar devastation, the nearby villagers had almost nothing to sustain them in the way of food, medicine, or help of any kind, and their suffering was terrible to witness. Jack shared that during this time he was exposed to some of the meanest men he'd ever met, two of whom were in his own company—men who didn't care if someone was hurt, even children. Jack said, "Fear and anger were everyday emotions. Especially at night. It was a living hell." His stories of the eighteen months he spent in South Korea impressed upon us the horrors of war and the importance of working together to find peaceful solutions to conflict.

Jack was greatly disturbed by his experience in South Korea, so much so that when he completed the two years of military service required by the draft (December 1956) he went back to Texas and enrolled himself in his old alma mater, the seminary at Southern Methodist University (SMU). He hoped the religious setting would help him find his peace.

In the course of his time at SMU, Jack met up with an old friend, Harry Craig, who had also served in the military in South Korea. The two of them went to their first Bahá'í fireside at the home of Raul Walls in Dallas. Soon thereafter, in March of 1959, Jack declared as a Bahá'í. A month later, he was studying and travel teaching with Ruth Moffett, one of the most dynamic Bahá'í teachers of the time. When he joined the Faith, Jack gave up his ordination as a Methodist minister and consequently his whole life was turned upside down. But he came out standing on his feet and was a fabulous teacher. I could listen to him all day long. He continued to serve the Faith in a variety of appointed and elected positions, including serving on the National Spiritual Assembly of the Bahá'ís of the United States.

Those are just a few examples of the fascinating people who graced our home, enriched our lives, and brought the world into our living room.

Dad's Travels

Dick Benson (the host of the first Bahá'í fireside / birthday party that I had originally stumbled into) quickly became close friends with my father, and the two of them did a lot of travel teaching together. If they had a few free hours, they'd hop in a car and drive until they found folks interested in hearing about the Faith. It was unusual to see a black man and a white man traveling together as friends, so sometimes, when the two of them would stop to talk to people who were working in, say, a cotton or tobacco field, the folks would run away at the sight of them. But usually they found people interested in hearing what they had to say.

Traveling in integrated company was always risky, even with my dad and Dick. I was with them on one trip in April of 1964 when the three of us went to Chicago for the Bahá'í National Convention. We got a late start, drove all night, and stopped for breakfast at a small diner in Corbin, Kentucky. It must have been around six in the morning because we were the first ones in the door. In those days, some restaurants would serve black people, and some wouldn't. It was the time of the civil rights movement—that period of change—and we were hoping for the best. The waitress seated us, took our order, and served us our food. Perhaps she assumed that all three of us were white. At any rate, shortly before we finished our meal, several white men came in together, and while they were eating, they kept looking over in our direction. They were staring specifically at my dad. After we'd paid the bill and were getting up to leave, one of the white guys came over to our table and said to my dad, "I've been watchin' you, and I've been wondering. Ain't you a colored fella?"

The comment was not a friendly "Welcome to Corbin" greeting. It was a threat. All eyes were on us. We were outnumbered and in danger.

My father took a deep breath and slowly responded with, "You know, I saw you watchin' me. I was watchin' you, too. And I was wonderin' the same thing. Aint *you* a colored fella?" Then, Dad pointed at the man and shouted, "Niggah! You better get outta here!"

The man jumped and made toward the door! Everybody looked confused. Dick started to laugh but quickly caught himself and threw his hand over his mouth. We zipped out of the diner and watched our backs as we drove away. We laughed about it in the car, but the situation could have turned out badly. Dad had handled the threat brilliantly. He deescalated the situation by disorienting people enough to get us out of the restaurant without incident.

I recently learned from my friend Louis Venters, a historian who teaches at Frances Marion University, that Corbin, Kentucky has a long history of fierce racism. In 1919, a white mob drove all of the black residents out of Corbin, and established itself as a "sundown town"—that is, an all-white town that prohibited non-whites from living there altogether. This bigotry was enforced through local laws, intimidation, and violence for most of the twentieth century.* If we'd known that Corbin was a sundown town, we probably would've driven past it and not stopped for breakfast 'til we hit Cincinnati.

It was nothing for my father to drive all over North Carolina, South Carolina, and Georgia to teach the Faith. People would set up firesides for him to speak at, and he'd be off—usually with me or one or two of my siblings in tow. In addition to his family, my father's passion was sharing the Faith. He was a superb teacher and a natural speaker.

One time early in their Bahá'í lives, my mother and father went to Georgia for a Bahá'í meeting. While they were sitting in the audience waiting for the program to begin, the master of ceremonies got up, made some brief comments, then said, "Now I will introduce our speaker for the evening, Mr. Charles Abercrombie." My father was shocked. In no way did he expect to be the speaker. But he got up, went to the podium, and started talking. When he finished, everyone applauded. As he got back to his seat, my mother took him by the hand and said, "Honey, that's the best talk I ever heard you give." He looked at her in astonishment and said, "What did I say?"

Dad had a way of explaining things that made spiritual concepts easy to understand. When describing the principle of progressive Revelation, he'd say something like, "You start in first grade, then you go to second grade. But when you're in second grade, you don't forget everything from first grade. You build on what you learned before. You still love your first-grade teacher, but you can't shut yourself off from what your second-grade teacher has to tell

---

* For more information on the history of Corbin, Kentucky, see this March 10, 2007 article from NPR: https://www.npr.org/templates/story/story.php?storyId=7772527.

you. In a similar way, as a Bahá'í, I love Jesus Christ. But I can't shut myself off from what the Return of the Divine Teacher has to tell me."

Another one of my father's analogies was: "You can't go from simple arithmetic to calculus. You study simple arithmetic, then you take algebra and geometry. When you've had those classes, then you're ready for calculus. And when you're in calculus, you don't throw away everything you learned in arithmetic, geometry, and algebra. You use it all to learn more. That's what progressive Revelation is like. When the Messenger of God comes, He gives you what you can handle at that time. After you've been in class long enough to understand, the Messenger comes again with more to teach."

One summer, Dad went to Chicago to speak at a Bahá'í public meeting that was held at the Trianon, a famous cultural dance venue located at East 62nd Street and Cotton's Grove on the southside of Chicago. The Trianon is massive ballroom with huge columns inside the building itself. My friend Smitty was there for the whole summer as part of a Bahá'í youth service project, and he admired how Dad worked the Trianon's columns into his talk. Dad said, "You see that column there? You don't know how far into the ground it goes. And you can't see how far it extends into the rafters. We know what we see here and now. And we Bahá'ís want to tell you what is happening here and now."

More than once, Dad traveled to the Chicago area to do masonry repair work on the Bahá'í Temple that sits on the shore of Lake Michigan. One of those visits prompted him to quit smoking. It was common for people in my father's generation to smoke cigarettes, and he had smoked since he was a teenager. But when he became a follower of Bahá'u'lláh, Dad was no longer comfortable with his habit. Bahá'í law does not forbid smoking, but the habit is identified as harmful. My dad wanted to quit smoking but had not yet managed to stop. So the way Dad told it, he was smoking a cigarette as he was working on the Temple steps, and when he got to the end of his smoke, he put the cigarette butt on the ground and stepped on it. Satisfied that the embers were snuffed out, he got back to work. A few minutes later, he noticed that the cigarette butt was still smoking, so he stepped on it again until he was positive that the cinders were absolutely extinguished. Then he got back to work. Shortly afterward, he noticed the cigarette butt was smoking *again*. He picked it up, tore it apart, buried the pieces in different spots, and never smoked another cigarette!

Dad had always made it clear that he would never ride in an airplane—that is, until the National Spiritual Assembly of the Bahá'ís of the United States asked him to go to the Bahamas to organize some youth programs. Dad had no desire to go to the Bahamas, but I didn't hear him object, not once. He bought a ticket, got on the plane, and flew to the Bahamas. The farthest he ever traveled for the Faith was Israel. In 1992, he flew to the Bahá'í World Center in Haifa, Israel to participate in the centenary commemoration of the Ascension of Bahá'u'lláh. The House of Justice had allotted a certain number of delegates to each national community, and my father was invited by our National Assembly to be one of the nineteen Bahá'ís who went from the United States. There's a video of the Ascension Commemoration that shows attendees from all over the world going up the partially completed steps and terraces that led to the Shrine of the Báb* on Mount Carmel, and you can see my father in that movie. He told us that going up all of those stairs was both a spiritual bounty and a penance!

Years later, on three different occasions, I would make the trip to the Bahá'í World Center and experience that bounty and penance for myself. By the time of my visits (1998, 2000, 2017) construction of the nineteen terraces leading up to as well as beyond the Shrine of the Báb were complete, and I was able to walk up all of them—over 1500 steps in an almost vertical climb of over half a mile. There are benches on each of the nineteen terraces, and I can tell you that I made use of all of them.

---

* The Báb, meaning "the Gate" was the Herald of Bahá'u'lláh. The Báb's remains are interred at the Bahá'í World Center in a Shrine on Mount Carmel.

- 12 -

Race Relations Pioneers

By the time I graduated from Sterling High School in June of 1964, more than a dozen of my schoolmates had embraced the Bahá'í Faith: Lawrence (Duke) Acker, Nolan Babb, Curtis Butler, Eddie Donald, Harry Johnson, Sandra Knuckles, Lawrence MacNeil, Steve Moore, Brenda Pension, Martha Shamley, William (Smitty) Smith, Ralph Sullivan, and Arthur Williams. Many adults joined as well. In response to our area's growth, the National Spiritual Assembly made Greenville one of the official sites for the 1964 Summer Youth Project.* The purpose of these projects was for youth to pray and study the Bahá'í writings together, carry out acts of service to both the Bahá'í and greater communities, teach the Faith, strive to demonstrate Bahá'í principles in everything we did, and build bonds of fellowship.

The project began with an orientation session at the Louhelen Bahá'í School Retreat and Conference Center in Davison, Michigan. In this training, the participants reviewed Bahá'í principles and the current teaching plan as well as protocols for how to be respectful guests for weeks at a time in in the homes of people who would be hosting them. (The latter included instructions to always accept what was offered at meals, finish all of the food on your plate, do more than your part of the chores, and keep shower time down to sixty seconds.) My father was one of the faculty members. After

---

* For more information on the 1964 Summer Youth Projects, see "Bahá'í News" Issues #401 (August, 1964), #403 (October, 1964), and #404 (November, 1964). https://bahai.works/Bahá'í_News.

orientation, the youth were given their city assignments. Several youth were assigned to Greenville, including Richard Thomas and my cousin Bo Jack (both of whom were black), along with Doug Ruhe, Patsy Sims, Jim Sims, Karl Borden, Ed Hockenbury, Marian Parmelee, and Laurie Cohen (all of whom were white).

Richard Thomas, who was from Detroit, was the oldest and most experienced participant in the Greenville project. He was twenty-five years old, had served in the Marines from 1957–1960, and had already begun his studies at Michigan State University. Richard hadn't spent much time in the Deep South, which I'm sure was intentional. He was aware of the South's overt hostility toward blacks, especially black men. But now here he was, assigned to spend the summer in Greenville, South Carolina.

The Greenville Bahá'ís had decided to host the visiting youth in a way that would foster unity in diversity. The black youth (Richard and Bo Jack) would be housed in a white home (the Bensons'), and the white youth (everybody else) would be housed in a black home (the Abercrombies'). The idea of staying in a white neighborhood, with all of its potential dangers for a black man and the people in the household that hosted him, made Richard nervous, so he talked about the situation with my father. "Mr. Abercrombie," he said, "I'm with this wonderful white couple, but we're in the Deep South. Can I stay at your house instead?" To Richard, this was a perfectly logical request and the only sensible thing to do. However, my father told him, "No, Richard. You gotta go back to the Bensons'."

Richard did go back to the Bensons', but that evening there arose yet another level of risk. As everybody was getting ready to retire for the evening, Joy told Richard and Bo Jack, "Sometimes Bahá'ís come through Greenville at night and they need a place to stay, so we leave the front door unlocked all night long." The prospect of being a black man staying in a white household in a white neighborhood with the front door unlocked all night long was almost more than Richard could bear. Some years later, he told me that he was so scared that when everybody else went to bed, he secretly made his way downstairs and locked the front door.

Then it got worse still. Richard had a free afternoon, so Joy asked him to go with her and her children for a picnic at a park. Richard thought that Joy had lost her mind. There was nothing rational about what she proposed—a black man accompanying a white woman at a public park—and he declined for safety reasons. But Joy explained to him, "This is what Bahá'ís do." He was nervous about it, but he went anyway, and they had a little interracial picnic in a park. He told me afterward, "The cars were slowing down, and people were staring at us. It was dangerous!"

We had a summer of rich relationship building. Jim and Patsy Sims were from Tennessee, and they both spoke in long Southern drawls that out-drawled even the South Carolinians. Jim and Patsy were personifications of the word "countrified." We used to tease Jim because he always walked around barefoot. We'd comment on his toes: "Jim, your toes are so far apart, your feet are so wide. What's up with that?" He'd slowly answer, "That's 'cause I grew up barefoot." Jim's father was a chemistry professor at Tennessee State University. Jim always had shoes—he just preferred not to wear them.

There are some negative stereotypes of white people with strong Southern drawls, but Patsy and Jim Sims didn't match any of them. Yet they talked the way they did. Now, I didn't know this at the time, but Richard Thomas later told me that he'd always wondered what he'd do if he ever met a really Southern white Bahá'í. He figured that would be the ultimate test of his faith. Well, the ultimate test of Richard's faith happened in our kitchen when he met Jim Sims. Richard showed no reaction but he thought, "Oh no. There's no way I can relate to this dude." He knew he was being tested. But then what happened is that with praying, studying the Bahá'í writings, and serving together over the weeks of the project, Richard and Jim became super close friends—lifetime friends. It was another affirmation that Bahá'u'lláh changes hearts.

No Place to Hide

In the youth's study that summer, we devoured *The Advent of Divine Justice* by Shoghi Effendi, a book we felt a special connection with because it addressed the American Bahá'ís specifically. In it, Shoghi Effendi described the basic ills afflicting American society, the probable course of world events, and the opportunities and challenges that all Americans would have to face in the near and distant future. He told how the world is "contracting into a neighborhood," how the destinies of all nations are interwoven, and how Bahá'ís can best rise to the challenge of contributing to the newly emerging global civilization.[1] We were all grateful to have the current corruptions explained, a hopeful vision of the future outlined, and productive tasks defined. Personally, I felt close to Shoghi Effendi because I had visited his gravesite in London and had looked at many of his original papers, maps, and personal effects.

Much of our study focused on racial prejudice, an issue addressed at length in *The Advent of Divine Justice*. A favorite passage, and one that all of us memorized, was "As to racial prejudice, the corrosion of which, for well-nigh a century, has bitten into the fiber, and attacked the whole social structure of American society, it should be regarded as constituting the most vital and challenging issue confronting the Bahá'í community at the present stage of its evolution."[2]

Of course, Shoghi Effendi hadn't just named racial prejudice as the most vital and challenging issue. He also specified things that blacks and whites had to do to contribute to its solution. For example, he stated that the task of white people is to abandon "their usually inherent and at times subconscious sense of superiority, to correct their tendency towards revealing a patronizing attitude towards the members of the other race, to persuade them through their intimate, spontaneous and informal association with them of the genuineness of their friendship and the sincerity of their intentions, and to master their impatience of any lack of responsiveness on the part of a people who have received, for so long a period, such grievous and slow-healing wounds."[3]

The task of black people, Shoghi Effendi described, is "through a corresponding effort on their part, show by every means in their power the warmth of their response, their readiness to forget the past, and their ability to wipe out every trace of suspicion that may still linger in their hearts and minds."[4]

And for both blacks and whites, he stated:

Let neither think that the solution of so vast a problem is a matter that exclusively concerns the other. Let neither think that such a problem can either easily or immediately be resolved. Let neither think that they can wait confidently for the solution of this problem until the initiative has been taken, and the favorable circumstances created, by agencies that stand outside the orbit of their Faith. Let neither think that anything short of genuine love, extreme patience, true humility, consummate tact, sound initiative, mature wisdom, and deliberate, persistent, and prayerful effort, can succeed in blotting out the stain which this patent evil has left on the fair name of their common country.[5]

There it was. No place to hide. We knew that achieving the realization of the oneness of humanity was going to be a long and difficult road, but the joy we felt in studying Shoghi Effendi's guidance and working together to embody the actions, qualities, and relationships necessary to cure the disease of racial prejudice was indescribably glorious!

Parks, Pools, and Sea Lions

As I mentioned previously, one of the objectives of the summer youth project was to be of service to the greater community; that is, to work together with like-minded people and organizations in activities that would benefit many folks in Greenville, regardless of their religious affiliations. While the needs in Greenville were many, choosing what to focus on in our service was easy. We wanted to engage with others in the promotion of race amity and social justice. So we looked to the civil rights activities that were happening in and around Greenville. It came to our attention that the Spiritual Assembly of Greenville was already monitoring a certain local civil rights issue that, we thought, was pretty bizarre. I have to take a moment to share the situation with you.

Although in 1954 the Supreme Court ruled segregation of public facilities to be unconstitutional, schools in Greenville County were still segregated in the early '60s. This was the case in much of the country, especially the South. In 1963, however, it became clear to everyone that avoidance of the federal law banning segregation would no longer be possible—that the law was actually going to be enforced by the federal government. School integration was inevitable, and so was the integration of other government-run facilities, such as public parks and recreational grounds. This meant that the way the local government did things had to change, and quickly.

The city of Greenville had long operated segregated public swimming pools: a swimming pool for blacks at Green Forest Park (behind the White-house Community Center) and a swimming pool for whites in Cleveland Park. In response to the apparently unthinkable prospect of integrating the pools and having black and white people swimming in the same water, the city council closed both pools. At first, city officials explained that the pools had been temporarily shut down for maintenance. However, it came to light that the city council had made a quiet arrangement with the Cleveland Park Zoo for the white swimming pool to become the new site of the zoo's sea lion exhibit. By the time of the youth project (summer of 1964), a public debate about the Cleveland Park pool was in full swing.

Members of the Greenville Spiritual Assembly had already joined with like-minded folks in appealing to the city council to establish both pools as integrated recreational facilities—for people, not animals. One of the members of the Bahá'í community—Bernice Williams, who spoke at a city council meeting—is recorded in the *Greenville News* as saying, "We all know why the pools were not opened this year, and it is a shame that for this reason we must sacrifice wholesome pleasures for our children for the sake of a few sea lions."* For months, there was public debate about what to do with the pools. The participants in the youth project didn't become directly involved in these debates since this was already being handled by the Greenville Assembly, but we did learn a lot about public discourse and the way things work as the Assembly shared its experience.

The issue eventually died down after city officials discreetly arranged for the Cleveland Park pool to be filled in with dirt and made into a garden. The

---

* For more information on Bernice Williams, and the desegregation of Greenville's Parks, see Venters, *No Jim Crow Church*.

pool just disappeared overnight. Sometime later, what had been the blacks-only pool at Green Forest Park was filled in, and the Whitehouse Community Center as well as the skating rink across the street were bulldozed. The Phyllis Wheatley Community Center, which had served the black community at its location in downtown Greenville for years, was relocated to Green Forest Park (about six miles from downtown on the edge of Nicholtown). The pool and skating rink were never rebuilt. Today, at both parks, it's impossible to tell where the pools had been.

Freedom Schools

As the youth gathered information on opportunities to assist with race amity and civil rights activities in Greenville, all possibilities were evaluated in terms of Bahá'í laws prescribing acceptable forms of behavior in social discourse and civic activity. These laws included absolute nonpartisanship, nonviolence, and obedience to government.* These were not mere suggestions for behavior. These laws were embedded in Bahá'í scripture, and, as followers of Bahá'u'lláh, we were bound to uphold their standards.

Our final decision on a service project, which the youth arrived at fairly quickly, was to offer our support to the local Freedom School program. Organized by the Student Nonviolent Coordinating Committee (SNCC), the Freedom Schools were all about education, community building, critical thinking, social consciousness, service, fellowship, and citizenship—all of which harmonized with what the Bahá'ís believe is the will of God for this age. The program was also nonpartisan, nonviolent, and operated under the laws of the land. For all of these reasons, it seemed to be the perfect choice for the youth's outreach program.

The local Freedom School organizers accepted the Bahá'í youth's offer to assist as volunteers. In fact, the organizers were thrilled. With the local Bahá'í

---

* For more information on Bahá'í laws regarding obedience to government and non-violence, see Peter Khan, comp., "Political Non-Involvement and Obedience to Government." 2003-01-12. http://bahai-library.com/khan_political_non-involvement_obedience.

youth in addition to the Bahá'í youth from out of town, we increased the Greenville Freedom School's manpower by over twenty people. They were also appreciative of the surprising integrated nature of our group, which added a different element (white people) to the Freedom School's personnel. All of the youth, black and white, served in an unpretentious fashion. The school organizers and staff were always warm and hospitable, and everybody was grateful for the opportunity to work together.

Among their services, the Freedom Schools helped prepare the black population for school desegregation. Greenville's plan for school desegregation was promising to be a slow process. In the summer of 1964, fifty-five black children (out of seventy-five applicants) were chosen to be transferred to all-white schools for the 1964–1965 school year.* The next year, more black students would be transferred. We called these children "little Davids against Goliath" because they would be entering a system that was hostile to colored people. While most blacks saw desegregation of the schools as a worthy goal for the purpose of making equitable resources available to all children, they also knew it would not be an easy process.

I've heard some journalists describe the purpose of the Freedom Schools as preparing black students for the stricter standards of white schools. I believe that is an erroneous statement. The state academic standards for black schools and white schools were the same. The immediate purpose of the Freedom Schools was to try to prepare black students and their families for the emotional, psychological, and social trauma of school integration—of having to closely associate with people who had been and still were hostile to colored people. To help blacks through this difficult time and to bolster everyone's courage, the Freedom School in Greenville offered a variety of educational and recreational activities for children, youth, and adults at a branch of the main

---

* For more information on the desegregation process in Greenville, SC, see "Memory, History, and the Desegregation of Greenville, South Carolina," in Moore and Burton, eds., *Toward the Meeting of the Waters: Currents in the Civil Rights Movement of South Carolina during the Twentieth Century.*

library, at Springfield Baptist Church (the largest black church in town), and also at the YMCA.

My time to engage with the Bahá'í youth that summer was somewhat limited because, having graduated high school in June, I had a full-time job at Steel Huddle Manufacturing Company, a foundry that made looms. (That was back when textile manufacturing was a major industry in upstate South Carolina.) But, happily, my work hours were from 6:00am to 2:30pm Monday through Friday, which left me free to engage in Bahá'í service, study, and fellowship in the afternoons, evenings, and weekends.

The first task that the Freedom School gave to the Bahá'í youth was to go door-to-door in the Fieldcrest and Nicholtown neighborhoods (two of the large black neighborhoods on our side of Greenville) to talk with families about what the program offered and to register people for classes. We did this on weekends and weeknights when parents would likely be home, so I was able to help. We divided up the neighborhoods into sections and went in teams of two or three to houses on our assigned streets. I think the fact that our teams were diverse in skin color and glowing with fellowship may have helped get people's curiosity up about what we had to share. Everyone we approached took the time to listen to the Freedom School information and seemed happy to get it. A lot of people registered themselves and their kids for the classes. As we went door-to-door, we also offered to help adults register to vote if they weren't registered already because voter registration was part of the Freedom School program.

Frankly, it was a lot of fun to walk the streets of Fieldcrest and Nicholtown, knock on doors, meet new people, and share the Freedom School's offerings. We were always politely received. Many people invited us inside their homes, offered us refreshments, and invited us to come back.

Once the Freedom School classes and recreational activities got started at the church and YMCA, the Bahá'í youth assisted as instructors and helpers. We also helped Richard Thomas with the Black History classes he taught at the library. These classes came about when the Freedom School organizers became aware of Richard's special interest and expertise in the subject. We were all in awe of Richard's knowledge. None of us—young or old, black or white—had known anything about African civilizations before hearing his presentations.

What's Going On?

The typical agenda for the youth in the service project was to get up early in the morning, gather to pray and study, and then serve the Freedom School most of the afternoon. The evenings and weekends held a variety of activities that included hosting Bahá'í devotionals, firesides, or study sessions, sharing information about the Faith with people who we would meet at parks or other locations, and visiting people who had expressed an interest in learning more about the Faith. We would do this in Greenville and also, by invitation, in other communities in South Carolina, North Carolina, and Georgia.

One of our teaching sites was Piedmont, South Carolina, a small rural town a little over twelve miles south of Greenville. Steve Moore (who was in my graduating class) lived there, and we had firesides and devotionals at his house. We had fun in his neighborhood and did a lot of teaching there. The unfortunate thing was that the integrated nature of our group was especially unappreciated in Piedmont.

It was an evening in July of 1964. Smitty, Patsy, Jim, and a couple of other youth who had helped Steve host a fireside at his home had just started to drive back to Greenville when their car broke down. They were trying to problem-solve the situation when some white people gathered around them, hurling insults about them being an integrated group. More white people gathered, they got louder and louder, and it began to look like a mob. Smitty told me that it was about to get "real ugly" when a white minister came by, saw what was happening, and called out to the crowd, "I'm a man of God! Get back and leave these people alone!" Maybe some of them were his parishioners—at least it was clear that he was well-known and respected—because the people actually did what he said. When the crowd dispersed, the minister went into a tavern and called somebody to help with the car. With the repairs made, the youth thanked their good Samaritan and got back to Greenville safely. The minister, whoever he was, truly came to their aid.

Later that week, at another gathering at Steve's home, the youth received death threats on the phone. All indications were that Steve's house and the people in it were going to be attacked. There was no incident that day, but these serious threats put some of the youth in the mindset that they needed to be armed with weapons for protection. Back in Greenville that evening, Dick Benson sat all of us down, listened to what was happening, and of course was concerned. Some of the youth wanted to get ready for a fight. But Dick was able to deescalate the situation and direct everyone to an appropriate nonviolent and no-weapons response. He reported the threat to local authorities, and he consulted with the National Spiritual Assembly as well. I'm not sure what all went on behind the scenes, but all the youth calmed down and continued with their activities despite the occasional threats.

It was a fact of the times that the integrated nature of Bahá'í groups attracted attention and was often dangerous. But sometimes we had fun with our out-of-the-ordinary appearance. That's what happened whenever Dad took some of us out on a construction job. The youth loved my dad. They called him "Poppa Jake." I don't even know where that name came from, but that's what they called him. Whenever possible, Dad gave the guys an opportunity to earn money by assisting with his masonry work during their free days. Often Doug Ruhe and Jim Sims were included in the mix. Dad would roll up to a work site with these white guys in his truck and then start giving them instructions: "OK Doug, get these bricks over there. Jim, I need that wheelbarrow. Quick now!"

Now my father was well respected in the community, but he was still a black man. At that time, whites just didn't work for blacks, and black people never told white people what to do. The other workmen on the site—white and black carpenters and other tradesmen—would just stare, jaws dropped, as if to say, "What's going on?!" Later on at my house, we'd all be rolling on the floor laughing about their shocked expressions.

After several weeks, the youth project came to a close and I was sorry to have to say good-bye to all of the out-of-towners. It got back to us that when Richard returned to Detroit and was telling his Bahá'í community about his experiences in Greenville, he said, "You know, you guys haven't been put to the test. The Bahá'ís in Greenville are really putting their lives on the line. You guys are talking about race unity, but the Bensons and the Abercrombies, they are incredible. They are race relations pioneers."

- 13 -

Moving On

One evening in the fall of 1964, I walked into Club DeLisa, a small restaurant and nightclub in Nicholtown just down the street from our house. The DeLisa served the best cooked shrimp in town and attracted people from all over. I'd been there many times, but as I entered the club that night, I spotted a young woman I'd never seen before—the beautiful Sara Cannon. In the course of the evening, I managed to speak with her. She was from Liberty, South Carolina, a town about thirty minutes outside of Greenville. At the end of the evening, I made a date to visit Sara at her home the next Saturday night.

Before our date, I put a good bit of time into polishing up my 1934 Ford. It was a strikingly unusual vehicle, and my plan was to impress Sara by driving up to her house in this shiny vintage car. What I hadn't planned on was that as soon as I got to her house, one of my car's spring supports broke, and Sara had to drive me back to Greenville in her car. That was embarrassing. But we still had a great time, and this first date became the start of a whirlwind romance.

Sara was an independent thinker and way smarter than I was. She was a registered nurse and had a full-time job at Greenville General Hospital. She lived with her parents in Liberty and most of her extended family—grandparents, aunts, uncles, and cousins—lived in the Liberty area, too. She had one sibling—a younger brother, Jacob Jr.—who was away serving in the Navy. Sara, her parents, and many of her extended family members attended New Hope Baptist Church, a black church in Liberty where her mother played the organ. Sara's dad and I got along just fine, and the fact that I was a Bahá'í didn't seem to faze him. Sara's mother was not as enthusiastic about her daughter dating a Bahá'í, but she was kind to me. Sara's heritage was at least as mixed as mine was, so we had that experience in common. Like the Abercrombies, her family members came in all different colors.

As for my parents, they admired Sara and were happy to see us together. Sara and I dated for a a couple of months and then announced that we wanted to get married. Both sets of parents blessed the union, and we were married shortly thereafter. Sara liked the Bahá'í wedding ceremony, so although she was Baptist, we were joined in matrimony with a Bahá'í service in the living room of my parents' home. My dad served as the master of ceremonies.

Sara's father was a long-distance truck driver and consequently was away from home a lot. Sara's mother did not like staying at home by herself, so after we got married, we lived with Sara's mother in Liberty whenever Father Cannon was out of town. That was about half the time. The rest of the time, we lived with my parents in Greenville. All of my older siblings were out of the house by then, and there was plenty of room upstairs for us to have our own private quarters.

My younger siblings Sherry, Beverly, and Phillip were delighted that Sara was now a member of the Abercrombie household. Beverly thought of Sara like a sister, and to this day, the two of them are very close. Phillip, who was eight years old when Sara and I got married, absolutely adored her and seemed to consider himself her guardian. One Saturday afternoon at the house, Sara and I were kidding around about something, and our jesting turned into loud, playful roughhousing. Phillip heard the commotion, burst into the room, and tackled me (he was half my size) hollering, "You'd better leave Sara alone!" She had to explain to him that we were just playing and that she was perfectly safe.

The difference in our religious affiliations was never an issue with Sara and me. When we were in Liberty, I would often accompany Sara and Mother Cannon to their church, and when we were in Greenville, Sara would often go with me to Bahá'í events. We also attended Bahá'í summer and winter schools together, including the particularly memorable Bahá'í school held at Penn Center in the winter of 1965.

I'd been attending Bahá'í summer and winter schools at Penn Center (on St. Helena Island in Beaufort County, SC) since Junie Faily took me to winter school there in 1962. The participants at these schools regularly filled the facility's lodging as well as the tents added by the organizers. The youth, of whom there were plenty, would sometimes travel across the bridge off the island to the little town of Beaufort, SC to shop, eat, or wash clothes at the laundromat. Typically, they would be an integrated group.

The particularly memorable part of the 1965 winter school occurred when the City Council of Beaufort sent a letter to Penn Center saying that colored people were welcome to come to Beaufort to do shopping, use the laundromat, and what have you, but that the city council did not want coloreds and whites coming to the city together in integrated groups. After reading the letter, the school committee presented the city council's request to the youth and asked them what they wanted to do about it. The youth, including Sara and I, consulted and decided that because the request was unjust and not supported by law, we did not feel obliged to honor the city council's request. And we didn't. For the rest of that school term, Sara and I and other young people continued to go into Beaufort in our normal integrated manner. We were all just enjoying good clean fellowship and living in God's Kingdom—which was frowned upon at the time.

After that winter school, the Regional Bahá'í Schools Committee tried to schedule Penn Center for the upcoming summer school, but it was not available on the dates we wanted. Consequently, the Schools Committee found a different site for the summer school—Camp Dorothy Walls, a conference and retreat center in Black Mountain, North Carolina, that had been the site of other Bahá'í events. A beautiful woodland setting with dormitory-style housing, Camp Dorothy Walls was a great place for a family school. This became even more important to me when, in June of 1966, Sara gave birth to our oldest child, James Richard, Jr. We've always called him Jamie. When I reflect on how it felt to be a new father, one word comes to my mind: *Joy!*

Jamie was a wonderful baby, so happy all the time. As a toddler, he'd wake up, hold onto the rails of his bed, and jump up and down laughing! Morning after morning, Sara and I would wake up to the sound of our child laughing. It just added to the beauty of life. By the end of 1969, Sara and I had two more children, Andrea Lavelle and Anita Elaine. The joy multiplied! That year we also packed up and moved to Michigan.

Leaving Home

Word got to me that Elizabeth and Robert (Bob) Martin, a black Bahá'í couple who lived in Adrian, Michigan, wanted to participate in the Deep South Project, a plan where teams made up of one black Bahá'í family and one white Bahá'í family would move into various communities in the South where there were no Bahá'ís. Through their fellowship and service together, these families would demonstrate Bahá'í principles and teach the Faith. The Martins wanted to be part of this project in Winnsboro, South Carolina. However, Bob owned a janitorial service in Adrian, and he needed someone to operate his business in his absence until he could sell it. The Martins also wanted to replace themselves with at least one Bahá'í so that the small Adrian community would continue to have enough adults to maintain a Local Spiritual Assembly. I had experience with janitorial work, so I went there to investigate the opportunity. Adrian was a small town—much smaller than Greenville—and I thought it had a nice feel to it. Within months, everything worked out. The Martins moved to Winnsboro, and Sara and I moved our family to Adrian.

Taking off to Michigan was a big deal for Sara and me. It was the first time that we were to live away from our hometowns and the first time we were to have a home of our own. Up to this point, we had been alternating between living in Greenville with my parents and living in Liberty with hers. Of course, one of our requirements before moving was to make sure that Sara's mother would be well attended to in the long spells when Father Cannon was on the road. A niece and a nephew had often stayed with her in the past, and we made arrangements with them to make sure that she would never be staying at the house alone. Mother Cannon was not what you might call a happy camper about our moving to Michigan, but she was safe and well cared for.

It was at once exciting and scary to be in a new town with no extended family or established network of friends. The Adrian Bahá'í community was small, as were most Bahá'í communities at that time, but it was also welcoming and a great help to our family. And it was in Adrian that Sara joined the Bahá'í community. She had been close to the Faith since before we were married, but through her own investigation, assisted by the Michigan Bahá'ís, she declared her belief in Bahá'u'lláh as the Word of God for today. Sara and I had always shared foundational spiritual principles and respected each other's beliefs. But now, engaging fully in the Bahá'í community as a family did have a special sweetness to it.

The Bahá'í community was well-regarded in Adrian. Still, I was surprised when one of our members, Don Carter, was elected to serve on the Adrian City Council. This was an unusual situation because although Bahá'ís are encouraged to be active and informed voting citizens, our guidance is to refrain from engaging in partisan politics. Bahá'ís seek to embody principles based on virtues and support these principles in public affairs, but do not affiliate with any political party, do not actively support one individual's candidacy over another, and are prohibited from campaigning for elected office. Don abided by these standards. Before the city council election, Don had simply declared in writing his eligibility to serve on the council and his willingness to do so, but he did not affiliate with a political party or do any campaigning. He had no posters or flyers or anything. He never said, "Vote for me."

Yet people voted for him. Like me, Don was an African American who worked in the janitorial field. He did not have financial or political clout. It was because a lot of people in Adrian knew Don and admired his good character that he was elected. He served admirably.

St. Joseph's

Before we were in Adrian a year, Bob Martin sold his business and I found other work. I got a full-time janitorial job at St. Joseph's Academy, a Catholic

K–12 boarding school that was associated with and on the grounds of Sienna Heights University. Bob Carter had told me about the vacancy and helped me secure the position. Both the academy and university were run by nuns who were members of the Dominican Order.

The academy campus that I worked at included a three-story building with classrooms and a cafeteria, and a separate three-story dormitory that housed all the girls who attended the school. Boys could also attend the academy as day students (they didn't live on campus), but only from kindergarten through eighth grade. In other words, once the boys reached puberty, they had to go to school someplace else. I was one of three janitors—the other two being women who had worked there for some time.

The position fit me well, and soon Sister Jean Cecile, the principal of the academy, promoted me to Director of Maintenance and Janitorial Services and gave me a substantial raise in pay. Shortly afterward, Sister Jean was called to the Mother House at the university campus for a conference with the mother superior and her council. When Sister Jean got back from the meeting, she called me to her office and told me the whole story.

Sister Jean had anticipated the reason why she had been called in—my hefty raise—so she had gone to the meeting with records of maintenance expenses before and after I'd worked at the school. It was clear that I'd saved the academy a ton of money. That was because I knew how to do electrical and plumbing work, I had been doing many of the smaller repairs myself, and whenever big jobs had required contracting a plumber or electrician, I had monitored their work. In the past, contractors had done unnecessary work and overcharged, and no one at the school had the expertise to recognize the deception. Sister Jean described the attitude of the mother superior and council members before they looked over the data (she may have used the word *vultures*), and how their demeaner changed after they saw that my employment was followed by a dramatic decrease in maintenance expenses. The numbers spoke for themselves. The mother superior was pleased with Sister Jean's decision and even told her to pay me an additional $50.00 a week!

In addition to building maintenance, I also helped St. Joseph's school with building projects. I remodeled what had been a room with a small raised stage into a classroom with a raised observation deck partitioned off by a wall with a one-way mirror. It became the first Montessori classroom at St. Joseph's. The observation deck was used in the training of teachers in Montessori methods. I gave the deck its own entrance so people could come and go and do their observations without disturbing the students. Our daughters, Andrea and Anita, attended Montessori classes there.

It seemed that many people were eager to learn about the Bahá'í Faith in Adrian, and this included people at my place of employment. Sister Jean was particularly interested in learning and sharing information about Bahá'u'lláh. Whenever she invited family or other visitors for lunch, she would always seat them with me and tell them to "ask Richard about his religion." Of course, I was delighted to teach her family and friends about the Faith. She openly shared with everyone that the only reason she did not join the Bahá'í community was because "I have been a nun too long to change." Sister Jean was in her seventies and it had long been her plan to live out her life under the care of the Dominican Order. Considering her position, she taught the Bahá'í Faith as much as she could.

Expectations

As for race relations, traveling to Adrian from the Deep South met my expectations because my expectations were not very high. I knew from what I had seen on the news over the years that there were racial problems in the North, just as there were in the South. Just two years earlier, Detroit had been the site of one of the bloodiest race riots of the twentieth century, and Adrian was only an hour's drive from Detroit. But the extreme prejudice, anger, and hostility that precipitated the revolt in Detroit did not characterize the little town of Adrian.

While predominantly white, Adrian had a noticeable African-American population, including many blacks who were quite well-to-do. Also, that area was historically connected to the Underground Railroad, that nineteenth-century network of safehouses used by slaves escaping the South to "free states" in the North. Several of the homes that had harbored slaves were in Birdsall, Michigan, just outside Adrian's city limits. Perhaps because of its involvement in the Underground Railroad, the area had a welcoming feel to it, at least on the surface, and I did not experience the in-your-face racism of the South.

Then again, this brought its own challenge—how does one respond to subversive racism? The kind that says one thing and means another? My antenna would pick up this unspoken prejudice, and my response had to be subtle, too. For example, a week or two after we arrived in Adrian, I was at a little corner store when the checkout guy looked me up and down and said, "I bet you're glad to be away from the South." Those words could be interpreted as friendly enough, but the way he said them—the turn of his mouth, everything about his body language, and the way he ignored me when I was ready to pay at the counter—said, "You're not welcome here." I responded by just making it a point not to shop at that store.

Just as the Abercrombies were a color oddity in Greenville, our family was an oddity in Adrian. Our daughters, Andrea and Anita, had blonde hair when they were little and very light complexions. But in the summertime, their skin tanned easily, and they would get quite a few shades darker. When they played in our front yard in the summertime, drivers would slow down to get a better look at them, or even stop their cars in front of our house and just stare. They were trying to figure out how these colored girls could have blonde hair. As often as this happened, in our front yard and other settings, it was not something that any of us ever got used to.

Sometimes people's confusion and curiosity about our heritage was comical. One evening I went to a private home to inquire about some old coins that had been advertised for sale. (I had a small coin collection. My prize pieces were a 1901 five-dollar gold coin and a 1909 Victor D. Brenner penny.) I rang the doorbell, and an elderly white woman answered the door. I asked about the advertised coins, but she just stared at me until finally she asked, "What race are you?" I took a deep breath and said, "Ma'am, I'm a little bit of everything." I could tell that this woman was really studying my hair which, at that time, was light brown and in the style of a big Afro. Then she asked, "You don't have any *sheep* blood in you, do you?"

I couldn't get mad at her. She was too old. I just had to laugh. I said, "Ma'am, I may have."

In addition to my full-time job at St. Joseph's, I also had my own part-time business doing contract janitorial work. One weekend, I needed some extra help for a large floor-cleaning job, so I recruited several men, white and black, to work for a couple of days. When one of the white guys learned that I had negotiated the cleaning contract and that he was, therefore, working for a black man, he dropped the cleaning equipment—right in the middle of the job—and left the building. I happened to run into him at a café a few weeks later, at which time I offered to pay him for the hours that he *had* worked. He said, "I don't want none of your money" and stomped off. All I could do was leave that alone. The racial climate in Adrian was more amicable than what I had experienced in the South, but I still had to contend with stuff like that, even at St. Joseph's—although there Sister Jean had my back.

As the maintenance and janitorial director at St. Joseph's, I was responsible for everything on campus except the kitchen and cafeteria. That area was managed by the Saga Corporation, a food service company contracted to operate the Sienna Heights University and St. Joseph's Academy cafeterias. Saga had its own kitchen staff responsible for cooking and cleaning. The Saga on-site director was a white guy named Hershel. Every once in a while, the Saga kitchen staff would neglect attending to the cafeteria trash and insinuate that my janitorial staff should take care of it. Of course, this caused problems, and it was on one of these mornings that I went to the academy's cafeteria to talk with Hershel to remind him of his staff's responsibilities.

Hershel and I did not have what you'd call a good relationship. He sat there at a cafeteria table and listened to what I had to say, but after I finished and had walked off I heard him call out, "All right, Shine." *Shine* was a derogatory term for colored people that some folks used back then. It was an insult, as bad as "Nigger." It came from the phrase "shoeshine boy." I turned around and asked, "What did you say?" He came back with, "I said, 'All right.'" I said, "No, you didn't." I raised my voice and he raised his.

Suddenly, Sister Jean, the principal, walked out from the teacher's dining room. Neither one of us knew anybody was in there. We froze. She pointed to Hershel's table and said, "Rick, sit down." I said, "I don't need to sit down." She said, "Yes, you do." I walked over to the table and she and I sat down with Hershel. Then Sister Jean said, "You two are going to have to figure out how to get along with each other, or I'm going to have to get rid of one of you." Then she looked directly at Hershel and said, "And Hershel, you need to know that Rick would be impossible to replace." She held her stare for a moment and then walked away.

That day had started badly, but it ended up pretty good. I never had a problem with Hershel or the kitchen staff after that conversation.

In the summertime, when all the students were on vacation, the Dominicans would hire additional janitorial help to get all of the summer cleaning done on both campuses, Sienna Heights University and St. Josephs. Windows and carpets were cleaned, floors waxed and polished, paint refreshed, and everything deep-cleaned. The cafeteria at St. Joseph's closed for the summer, but the university cafeteria stayed open to provide lunch to the permanent staff and temporary help. At lunchtime, the white workers would sit at one table and the black workers would sit at another.

One lunchtime, after I'd gotten my tray of food, I noticed that the black table was full but that there was an empty space at the white table. So I walked up to the white table, greeted everybody, and sat down, not thinking much about it. One of the white guys, Larry, quickly picked up his food and left with an attitude of disgust. He wasn't going to sit and eat with a black. One of the other white workers whispered to me, "You have to watch out for him. He's a real racist, and his brother is even worse." I never had cause to sit at the white table again.

Years later, I walked into a restaurant in Adrian and saw him sitting at a table with a young boy. I took a seat at a table a good distance from them. But then the two of them came over to my table. Larry greeted me in a friendly manner and introduced the boy as his son. Then he said to his son, "I want you to meet Mr. Abercrombie. I was honored to work with him at St. Joseph's." We exchanged pleasantries, and that was that. Later, I found out that his sister was dating a black guy and that he and Larry had become close friends. Larry had made a turnaround. That's often what happens when, as they say, you've got skin in the game.

- 14 -

Out of Chaos

By the time Sara and I moved our family to Adrian, James Brown's recording, "Say it Loud—I'm Black and I'm Proud," had been popular for about a year. As I've been telling my story in these pages, I've been using the term *black* because that's how I talk now, but before that song became popular, to call someone *black* was fightin' words. *Negro* was OK, and *colored* was OK. *Black* was an insult.

By 1969, however, the colored community was celebrating blackness, and there was a new spirit of assurance. The Civil Rights Act of 1964 outlawed discrimination based on race, color, religion, sex, or national origin and, among other provisions, prohibited racial segregation in schools, employment, and public accommodations. At the same time, it was clear that actually ending entrenched segregation would be a long struggle. Civic laws had changed, but hearts had not.

The decade of the 1960s also saw heightened black anger at continued economic and social oppression. The dire consequences of racial prejudice, described decades earlier in the Bahá'í writings, were evident: "'If this matter remaineth without change, enmity will be increased day by day, and the final result will be hardship and may end in bloodshed.'"[1] From 1964 to 1969, more than a hundred American cities had been torn apart by race riots.

The history of the American Bahá'ís showed an eagerness to engage with others in the promotion of human rights, including participation in many activities of the civil rights movement. My brother Charles Jr. participated in nonviolent civil rights demonstrations in various places, including the first

Nashville sit-ins early in the 1960s. These sit-ins were appeals for equal rights that involved peacefully occupying space in racially segregated businesses or institutions. When Charles was a part of the sit-ins, they were very organized and systematic. If you wanted to participate, first you had to go to the training sponsored by the organizers, where you got instruction and practice on how to conduct yourself while engaging in nonviolent demonstrations. Training was required because it is painfully difficult to remain peaceful when you are being violently attacked.

In one instance, Charles was in a sit-in at a lunch counter where waiters, equipped with gas masks for their own protection, poured straight ammonia on the countertop in an attempt to displace the protestors. The passive demonstrators would be hit, kicked, and thrown around, as well as attacked and bitten by dogs. The organizers of the sit-ins had lawyers set up beforehand because they knew that all of the protesters would be arrested and taken to jail.

The protestors, drawing on their commitment, training, and the trust developed during that training, found the strength to remain calm in these brutal situations. They knew what goal they were working for and who they were working with. Charles told me that whenever he and his cohorts were thrown in jail, they would sing to keep up their courage. He said that one time their jailers were so moved by their singing that the jailers themselves made song requests! When he and others were arrested after a particular Nashville sit-in, the parents of the protesters, as well as people from the surrounding black community, brought so much food for the protesters that the jailers were jealous. My point here is that the sit-ins he was a part of in the early '60s were carefully orchestrated. Charles and the other protestors knew the sit-in organizers and the community they were operating in, the participants were trained, and they trusted each other.

But by 1969, things were so chaotic that it was not always easy to know who was in charge of a particular demonstration, what the objectives were, or whether the participants had been trained. The number of groups supporting the cause of civil rights was astonishing. For example, there was the

Organization of Afro-American Unity (OAAU); the National Association for the Advancement of Colored People (NAACP); the American Negro Labor Congress (ANLC); the Brotherhood of Sleeping Car Porters (BSCP); the Universal Negro Improvement Association (UNIA); the Nation of Islam (NOI); the Black Panther Party (BPP); the Congress for Racial Equality (CORE); the Fellowship of Reconciliation (FOR); the Student Non-Violent Coordinating Committee (SNCC); the Urban League; the Southern Christian Leadership Conference (SCLC); the Black Awareness Coordinating Committee (BACC); and the followers of Malcolm X. And there were spin-offs of many of those groups. But while they all professed to be working for the best interests of colored people, they didn't all work with each other or agree on goals and strategies. The danger for my Bahá'í friends and me was that in our enthusiasm to work toward civil rights through affiliation with one or more of these groups, we might fall in with activities that were contrary to the teachings of the Faith.

As I'd mentioned before, a Bahá'í approach to working for civil rights centers around the spiritual truth that humanity is one and requires absolute nonviolence. Bahá'í scripture states, "O ye lovers of God! In this, the cycle of Almighty God, violence and force, constraint and oppression, are one and all condemned."[2] Some of the groups mentioned above did espouse and enforce strict nonviolence, but not all. Also problematic was that although the leaders of a demonstration might be sincere in their intent to remain nonviolent, there was always the possibility that the event would turn violent through the undisciplined actions—or outright sabotage—of a few.

Decisions

Adrian was not a hotbed of protests, but I did get requests to participate in marches, sit-ins, and demonstrations held in other towns, particularly Detroit. These invitations came from friends who were affiliated with or sympathetic to some of the organizations named above. At first, I was torn over how to respond. On the one hand, I was the sole breadwinner of a family of five. I worked a full-time job during the week and did private contract work on most weekends. I didn't have time to participate in demonstrations, marches, and protests. On the other hand, I knew that progress toward justice would help my family in the long run. I wanted to be in the forefront of working with others for positive change, and it was tempting to go off and do what so many other people were doing. I had enjoyed working with the SNCC Freedom Schools in Greenville years earlier, and I knew it was possible to embody Bahá'í principles in worthy efforts to advance racial equality in the greater community.

A combination of two things ultimately made me decide to decline requests to join demonstrations. First and foremost was the effectiveness of Bahá'í activities that were successfully bringing people of all backgrounds together. Bahá'í priorities at that time included sharing Bahá'u'lláh's teachings through firesides and study groups, providing spiritual education to children, offering Bahá'í devotionals, developing the unique Bahá'í Administrative Order, inviting others into these activities, and striving to do all these things while embodying Bahá'í principles. None of these were small tasks, nobody on the planet was going to do them except followers of Bahá'u'lláh, and I had witnessed the power of these activities to change hearts, overcome racial divides, and build communities that shone as models of unity in diversity.

The second reason why I decided to decline invitations to engage in civil rights demonstrations was, as I've mentioned, the difficulty of figuring out whether or not any particular event harmonized with the teachings of the Faith. Who was really in charge? What were their real goals? Bahá'ís are not against anybody. We support the principles of justice and unity. Was a particular demonstration calling for justice? Or was it merely demonstrating against a certain politician, political party, or institution? Was the real intent of a certain group to just replace one kind of oppression with another? Was the motivation solely to tear down old ways of doing things? How could I know for sure? I understood from my study of *The Advent of Divine Justice* that social structures built on faulty principles *were* crumbling all by themselves and that this process of disintegration did not require my assistance.

For the above reasons, and considering my work schedule, I chose not to engage in civil rights demonstrations but to devote my time to building up an alternative to the decaying old order. Martin Luther King had spoken of the vision of "the Beloved Community."* I felt that, as a Bahá'í, I was actively building the Beloved Community and providing proof that it could succeed.

My decision relieved me of the risk of getting involved in activities that could be contrary to the Faith. But I was worried for some of my Bahá'í friends and family who were active in civil rights work. These included Smitty and Steve, friends I had taught the Faith to years earlier. I knew they were involved full-time in civil rights work in Greenville. My cousin Bo Jack was aggressively working civil rights strategies in Detroit. And my friend Richard, who I had first met when he came to Greenville for the youth service project in 1964, was active in civil rights work at Michigan State University. I knew their sincerity as Bahá'ís; that wasn't the issue. My fear was that the intensity of their activist work, combined with the large number of people and organizations that they worked with, plus the chaos of the time could land them in situations that violated Bahá'í principles.

Multiple Invitations

The National Spiritual Assembly of the Bahá'ís of the United States was concerned for the entire Bahá'í community during this tumultuous time, but it was especially anxious for the youth—those most likely to get involved in radical movements. One of the steps the Assembly took was to invite Bahá'í youth—certain young people from all over the country who had shown a desire to be at the vanguard of the civil rights movement—to meet with the Assembly at its headquarters near Chicago for an entire weekend. The purpose of the retreat would be to consult on Bahá'í involvement in civil rights activities, to listen to the challenges that these youth were experiencing in their individual circumstances, to consult on choices, and to provide guidance. I was happy when I learned about this meeting and even happier when I found out that my cousin Bo Jack and my friends Smitty, Steve, and Richard would be attending.

---

* See The King Center, "The King Philosophy." https://thekingcenter.org/king-philosophy/.

It seems that the youth who were invited to this meeting were identified by virtue of information that came to the National Assembly through at least a couple of channels—one being personal relationships. For example, certain Assembly members, such as Dr. Firuz Kazemzadeh and Mr. Glenford Mitchell, had conducted youth conferences throughout the 1960s. They personally knew youth such as Bo Jack and Richard, and they knew these guys wanted to be on the front lines of the civil rights movement. In this case, the invitation by the National Assembly felt like a continuation of a conversation. Another channel of information came through requests from Local Spiritual Assemblies for assistance on how to guide certain youth in their localities. This was the case for Smitty and Steve, my friends in Greenville.

Smitty had been drafted into the Army in the mid-1960s, served his two years in Vietnam, and then returned to Greenville upon his discharge. Soon after his return, he and Steve Moore established a Black Awareness Coordinating Committee (BACC) office in downtown Greenville across the street from the Ice Plant. They organized a variety of civil rights activities, including sit-ins just blocks away at Walgreens. These sit-ins protested the store's policy of refusing to seat and serve colored people at the store's lunch counter.

Early in 1969, it came to Dad's attention that Smitty and Steve kept weapons at the Greenville BACC office. Dad was worried about what this might mean for Smitty and Steve's ability to conduct their civil rights work in a fashion that accorded with Bahá'í principles of absolute nonviolence in civic affairs. Dad, who was the chairman of the Local Spiritual Assembly of Greenville, invited Smitty and Steve to meet with the Assembly to discuss their work and the weapons.

Smitty and Steve met with the Greenville Assembly, but the two of them were not what you would call "receptive" about the Assembly's cautionary advice. They confirmed they had weapons at the BACC office—an M1 rifle from Steve's father and a pump shotgun from Smitty's dad. They explained that they kept them at the office purely for defensive purposes and saw no need to remove them. Smitty later told me, "We accused the Assembly members of being timid people of the old order and told them that they didn't understand the revolutionary zeal of the day."

After the meeting, the Greenville Spiritual Assembly continued to be concerned for my two friends, so Dad got in touch with the National Spiritual Assembly for guidance. In response, the National Assembly sent one of its members, a young white man, to Greenville to talk in person with Smitty and Steve. The three of them met at the BACC office. Smitty and Steve started the conversation by bombarding the National Assembly member with questions such as: "Have you been involved in the civil rights movement? Have you ever stood in a picket line? Have you spent time in jail for protesting segregation?" The Assembly member's response to all of their questions was, "No." Smitty replied, "Then you do not understand the plight of the people and we have nothing to talk about. This meeting is over." The Assembly member thanked Smitty and Steve for meeting with him, and left Greenville. Later in life, shaking his head over the rudeness that he and Steve had shown—first to the Local Assembly and then to the National Assembly member—Smitty admitted that, at the time, he and Steve were "equal opportunity disrespecters of authority."

The National Assembly responded by sending another one of its members to Greenville. This is how Smitty described it: "A few weeks later, I get home and see this guy sitting on the front porch with my mother. The two of them were talking, laughing, and having a good old time. I'm thinking, 'Is this guy selling insurance or something?' He had an olive complexion. My mother says, 'Smitty, I'd like you to meet Mr. Firuz.'" The visitor was Firuz Kazemzadeh, a professor of history at Yale University (he'd received his Ph.D. at Harvard) and a member of the National Assembly of the Bahá'ís of the United States. His heritage was Persian and Russian.

Dr. Kazemzadeh greeted Smitty warmly and said, "The National Assembly got your reply and asked me to meet with you. When can I come to your office and talk with you about your civil rights work?" A meeting was scheduled for the next morning. Meanwhile, Dr. Kazemzadeh enjoyed fellowship with Smitty's family throughout the remainder of the evening.

Maybe his parents' warm hospitality to "Mr. Firuz" had a tempering effect on Smitty's attitude. Whatever the reason, the meeting the next day was very productive. Dr. Kazemzadeh listened carefully to Smitty and Steve's concerns, goals, and strategies in their civil rights work. Later, Smitty told me, "Steve and I felt that Dr. Kazemzadeh respected us as people. He truly saw us as equals and was willing to hear our arguments. And his profound understanding of current events, the history behind them, and the road forward was undeniable. Steve and I were deeply interested in what he had to say." The three of them talked into the afternoon.

At the end of the meeting, Dr. Kazemzadeh invited Smitty and Steve to come to the National Assembly headquarters in Wilmette, Illinois to continue the discussion with the National Assembly, as well as with other youth from around the country. He explained that the Assembly had arranged for places for them to stay and that they would be the Assembly's guests. Smitty said that he and Steve were at first reluctant about the idea of going to Wilmette for such a meeting. But when Dr. Kazemzadeh named other activist youth who would be attending, such as Bo Jack Mangum, Richard Thomas, Ernestine White, and Robert Henderson, they accepted the invitation.

Validated and Invigorated

A few weeks later, Smitty, Steve, Bo Jack, Richard, and about fifteen other Bahá'í youth from all over the country were assembled at the National Bahá'í Center to meet with the National Assembly for a whole weekend. The meeting generated great excitement in the Bahá'í community. The Detroit Bahá'ís called it the "Badasht Conference on Race Relations."* I was working during that weekend, but I could think of nothing other than what might be happening with my friends and the National Assembly.

After the retreat, news of the gathering came quickly. I took the time to get in touch with my friends to get their firsthand reports. Bo Jack shared that the

---

* The Conference of Badasht (1848) was a significant conference in the early days of the Bahá'í Faith that, for the most part, involved young adult believers. It was at the Conference of Badasht that Táhirih, the greatest heroine of the early days of the Faith, chose to appear without her face veil and proclaimed the emancipation of women.

National Assembly and youth had reviewed Bahá'í scripture and authoritative guidance mandating nonpartisanship, absolute nonviolence, and adherence to the law of the land and the implications of these Bahá'í laws in civil rights work. They explored the importance of unity in diversity as a foundation for social transformation. While evaluating the benefits and risks of joining forces with particular civil rights groups, the youth found that the Assembly members were a rich source of experience. The advantages and potential dangers of using various activist strategies posed by non-Bahá'í organizations were assessed, and practical guidance was offered.

In their consultation with the National Assembly, the youth aired concerns they had about working within the Bahá'í community itself. These included generational issues. Many of the youth expressed impatience with the older black generation's worry that gains in racial amity that had been made slowly over the years might be lost if the black youth were too demanding. And the difficulties of discussing race relations within the Bahá'í community itself were voiced. How could the community move forward, the youth wanted to know, when many white Bahá'ís were blind to the reality of racial oppression as well as blind to their own prejudicial attitudes and actions? The Assembly advised the youth on how to have frank and loving consultation on such issues in their local communities.

In brief, the youth felt that the National Assembly heard and attended to all of their challenges and concerns. Smitty told me he was overwhelmed by the love that was manifest to all the youth during that conference. He said, "The Assembly members actually listened to what we had to say! It wasn't about getting us there to instruct us on the proper way to do things. The Assembly was concerned about what our issues were and offered alternative strategies for our consideration."

All the youth came away with more insights about civil rights leadership as well as a greater understanding of the Faith, the ability of Bahá'í institutions to provide guidance, and the power of Bahá'u'lláh to open hearts. The conference inspired Smitty, Steve, Bo Jack, Richard, and others to cease and desist their associations with organizations and individuals whose aims and strategies were too questionable. They all realigned their efforts and continued working as civil rights activists in ways that upheld the principles of the Bahá'í Faith.

In the weeks that followed, as those who had attended the retreat shared their new learnings and insights, we all grew in understanding. The youth who wanted to be at the vanguard of the civil rights movement—that is, to serve in leadership positions of positive social action in the greater community—got the guidance and support they needed to enhance and sanctify their service through the application of Bahá'í principles and adherence to Bahá'í law. Their eyes were also opened to the transformative and lasting effects of engaging with others in Bahá'í spiritual education, study, prayer, service, fellowship, and the strengthening of the Bahá'í Administrative Order.

And as for me, the reports I heard from Bo Jack, Smitty, Steve, and Richard confirmed my decision to work toward social progress by using what time I had to teach people about Bahá'u'lláh and walk with them on the path of spiritual education and service offered by the Bahá'í community. As the new year of 1970 approached, all of us felt validated, invigorated, and eager to follow our paths in light of Bahá'í guidance.

- 15 -

Reflections

It's been half a century since the events depicted in these pages. A lot has happened over those years. The Abercrombies have grown not only in number but in most every measure of diversity, capacity, complexity, and service to humanity in the United States and abroad. But that's another story. I'd just like to say that I love them all.

Sometimes I think about how my life would have been had I not become a Bahá'í. I suspect that either I would have landed in prison or been killed at a young age. Finding the Bahá'í Faith gave me the opportunity to experience my life with hope and joy. That's not to say that I've been free from the pain of learning. When I look back over my life, there are many moments that I wish I could rewind and redo. But I am always grateful for the moment in which I was inspired to investigate the Bahá'í Faith and to open my heart to Bahá'u'lláh's blessings and protections.

By 1997, the Greenville Bahá'í community had grown to the point where it was able to purchase a property for use as an official Bahá'í Center. Renovation of the building took over a year, and the formal dedication took place in January of 1999. It was especially poignant that the first big event held at that center was the reception after my father's funeral service in February of 1999.

My mother and father had been married over sixty years. When Dad died, my mother grieved day and night for months until she had a significant dream. As she told it, in her dream my father appeared to her and lovingly said, "Lillie, you have to stop your grieving because your grief is disturbing my soul." This powerful message consoled my mother, and she did stop grieving. She continued to cheer and inspire those around her until her passing in March of 2016. Both my mother and father are buried in the family cemetery plot next to the graves of John Marion, his wife Elizabeth, and a host of Abercrombie ancestors.

Now it's autumn of 2019 and, once again, I'm sitting on the front porch of 8 Rebecca Street. I look to the right and I can still see Biggie flying off the porch toward Melvin. I can still hear my father's booming voice echoing from inside and my mother laughing with delight. My parents joyfully served the Bahá'í Faith until their last breaths.

I've heard people say that the ability to recognize the station of Bahá'u'lláh is a gift given because of something that person did or would do that made him or her deserving of such a bounty. For years, I wondered what I may have done or would do to deserve that gift. But I've come to think that it wasn't anything I'd done at all. It was my parents who were deserving of such a bounty. And in order to deliver that gift, I think that divine Providence got my parents' attention by taking their hopelessly delinquent fifteen-year-old and transforming him overnight. It was a miracle for which I am daily grateful.

Sometimes people ask me how I feel about the state of the world today. In brief, I feel hopeful. The social disintegration foretold by Bahá'u'lláh can be seen all around us, but I am blessed to have eyes to see the integration that He stated would happen at the same time. Any gardener will tell you that the most beautiful and hardy plants grow out of the compost heap. As divisions between people get wider and uglier, I hear the calls for unity getting stronger, becoming more numerous, and coming from unexpected directions. People everywhere are crossing traditional lines of separation—racial, religious, and otherwise—and working together for humanity's common good. I think it is evident that we are witnessing the birth pangs of a global civilization whose watchword is unity in diversity. I am fortunate to be part of the Bahá'í community as it consciously strives to contribute to this emerging new reality.

Here we are on this planet, a speck in the universe, spinning a thousand miles an hour and headed to who knows where. This is surely a situation in which we all need to work in unity. And we can. I say this confidently because since the beginning of my own transformation in 1961, I have met Bahá'ís from all over the world who are experiencing the joy of coming together in unity for the spiritual, social, and material well-being of themselves and the greater community. I've also been fortunate to witness firsthand the positive effects of the Faith's approach to social transformation, not only in South Carolina and Michigan but also in Africa and India.

In January of 2000, I was part of a group of black men who went to several African countries at the request of the Universal House of Justice for the purpose of being of service to the National Spiritual Assemblies of those countries and encouraging the Bahá'í friends. My time was spent in Uganda and Ethiopia. And in the spring of 2016, I went with my sister Beverly to India where we met scores of Bahá'ís while visiting the Bahá'í Temple in New Delhi. This book is not the place to tell the stories of those trips. (Although, I have to at least mention the peril and pain of riding for hours through the remote African bush on the back of a bicycle with one hand clutching my suitcase and the other hand clutching the guy who was pedaling the bike. And how hard I laughed when my sister Beverly had to kiss an elephant in India.)

But I will tell you that in both of those trips I saw Bahá'í teachings challenging old prejudices and enabling people to build communities based on equity, inclusion, and empowerment. If the impact of the Bahá'í approach to social transformation throughout the world interests you, I suggest you watch the "Frontiers of Learning" video at https://www.bahai.org/frontiers/. In this documentary, you will see how new kinds of communities—inspired by the teachings of Bahá'u'lláh—are coming together in India, Columbia, the Democratic Republic of the Congo, and Canada. The accounts in the film are given in the people's own words.

I hear a lot of discouragement in the world, but I never feel discouraged. I see all of the world's affairs—the joy and the pain—as leading to the maturity of the human race. As a Bahá'í, I understand this verse of the Lord's prayer, "Thy Kingdom Come, Thy Will be done on earth as it is in heaven," as not only a prayer but also as a promise—a promise that will be realized. The human race is in the process of learning how to build the Kingdom of

God on Earth. And even if we have to get there by taking two steps forward and one step back, I believe we are blessed to be able to participate in this divine enterprise.

Ya Bahá'u'l-Abhá! Ya Bahá'u'l-Abhá! Ya Bahá'u'l-Abhá!

"O Thou the Glory of the Most Glorious!"

"O Thou the Glory of the Most Glorious!"

"O Thou the Glory of the Most Glorious!"

Richard Abercrombie
October 29, 2019

Notes

3 / Listening

1. Bahá'u'lláh, *Gleanings from the Writings of Bahá'u'lláh*, no. 122.
2. Bahá'u'lláh, The Kitáb-i-Aqdas, ¶182.
3. Bahá'u'lláh, *Gleanings from the Writings of Bahá'u'lláh*, no. 117.
4. 'Abdu'l-Bahá, quoted in "Two Wings of a Bird: The Equality of Women and Men," a statement written by the National Spiritual Assembly of the Bahá'ís of the United States, ¶16.
5. Bahá'u'lláh, *The Tabernacle of Unity*, ¶1.15.
6. Bahá'u'lláh, The Kitáb-i-Aqdas, ¶182.
7. Matthew 24:30.

4 / Inquisitions and Confirmations

1. Revelation 3:12.
2. 1 Corinthians 15:51–53.
3. John 14:6.
4. Exodus 24:2.
5. Bhagavad Gita 18:66.
6. Dhammapada 20:274.
7. Bahá'u'lláh, *Gleanings from the Writings of Bahá'u'lláh*, no. 90.2.
8. For more information on Penn Center and Bahá'í use of that campus, see Venters, *No Jim Crow Church*, pp. 199, 223–24, 224–25, 226; Venters, *A History of the Bahá'í Faith in South Carolina*, pp. 57, 58, 68, 69, 105.

5 / "You Get Off that Tractor"

1. Matthew 3:11.
2. 'Abdu'l-Bahá, *Abdu'l-Bahá in London*, pp. 92–93.

6 / Strange Looks

1. Bahá'u'lláh, The Kitáb-i-Aqdas, ¶72.
2. 'Abdu'l-Bahá, *Paris Talks*, no. 40.19–21.

7 / There and Back Again

1. Bahá'u'lláh, The Kitáb-i-Íqán, ¶196.
2. John 14:9.
3. John 14:28.
4. John 1:18.

8 / Bahá'í World Congress

1. Shoghi Effendi, *Messages to the Bahá'í World 1950–1957*, p. 127.

9 / Biggie

1. Isaiah 9:6–7, 11:14.
2. 'Abdu'l-Bahá, *Promulgation of Universal Peace*, pp. 277–81.
3. Isaiah 42:21.
4. 'Abdu'l-Bahá, *Promulgation of Universal Peace*, pp. 277–81.

12 / Race Relations Pioneers

1. Shoghi Effendi, *The Advent of Divine Justice*, ¶85.
2. Ibid., ¶51.
3. Ibid., ¶58.
4. Ibid.
5. Ibid.

14 / Out of Chaos

1. 'Abdu'l-Bahá, quoted in Shoghi Effendi, *The Advent of Divine Justice*, ¶56.
2. 'Abdu'l-Bahá, *Selections from the Writings of 'Abdu'l-Bahá*, ¶129.11.

Bibliography

Works by Bahá'u'lláh

Gleanings from the Writings of Bahá'u'lláh. Translated by Shoghi Effendi. Wilmette, IL: Bahá'í Publishing, 2005.

The Kitáb-i-Aqdas: The Most Holy Book. 1st pocket size edition. Wilmette, IL: Bahá'í Publishing, 1993.

The Kitáb-i-Iqan: The Book of Certitude. Translated by Shoghi Effendi. Wilmette, IL: Bahá'í Publishing, 2003.

The Tabernacle of Unity: Bahá'u'lláh's Responses to Mánikchí Sáhib and Other Writings. Haifa: Bahá'í World Center, 2006.

Works by 'Abdu'l-Bahá

'Abdu'l-Bahá in London: Addresses & Notes of Conversations. London: Bahá'í Publishing Trust, 1987.

Selections from the Writings of 'Abdu'l-Bahá. Wilmette, IL: Bahá'í Publishing Trust, 2010.

Works by Shoghi Effendi

Messages to the Bahá'í World 1950–1957. Wilmette, IL: Bahá'í Publishing Trust, 1971.

The Advent of Divine Justice. New ed. Wilmette, IL: Bahá'í Publishing Trust, 2006.

Other Works

"Bahá'í News" Issues #401 (August, 1964), #403 (October, 1964), and #404 (November, 1964). https://bahai.works/Bahá'í_News.

Etter-Lewis, Gwendolyn and Richard Thomas, eds. *Lights of the Spirit: Historical Portraits of Black Bahá'ís in North America, 1898–2000.* Wilmette, IL: Bahá'í Publishing Trust, 2006.

Moore, Winfred B. and Orville Vernon Burton, eds. "Memory, History, and the Desegregation of Greenville, South Carolina," in *Toward the Meeting of the Waters: Currents in the Civil Rights Movement of South Carolina during the Twentieth Century.* Columbia, SC: University of South Carolina Press, 2010.

National Public Radio. "Kentucky Town Re-Examines Its Racial History." March 10, 2007. https://www.npr.org/templates/story/story.php?storyId=7772527.

National Spiritual Assembly of the Bahá'ís of the United States. *Two Wings of a Bird: The Equality of Women and Men.* 1997. https://www.bahai.org/documents/nsa-usa/two-wings-bird.

"Political Non-Involvement and Obedience to Government." Compilation by Peter Khan, 2003-01-12. http://bahai-library.com/khan_political_noninvolvement_obedience.

The Bhagavad Gita: Introduced and Translated by Eknath Easwaran. Tomales, CA: Nilgiri Press, 2007.

The Dhammapada: Easwaran's Classics of Indian Spirituality, Book 3. Tomales, CA: Nilgiri Press, 2007.

The Holy Bible: Containing the Old and New Testaments. King James Version. Nashville: Thomas Nelson Publishers, 1989.

"The King Philosophy." https://thekingcenter.org/king-philosophy/.

Venters, Louis. *No Jim Crow Church: The Origins of South Carolina's Bahá'í Community.* Gainesville: University Press of Florida, 2015.

———. *A History of the Bahá'í Faith in South Carolina.* Charleston, SC: The History Press, 2019.

The Abercrombie family, circa 1962.
Left to right back row: Charles Jr., Melvin, Della, Charles Sr.,
Lillie, Harold, Ricky, Sherryfield. Front row: Beverly, Phillip.

John Marion Abercrombie (husband of Elizabeth) circa 1866.

Elizabeth Abercrombie (wife of John Marion) circa 1866.

Taken at the front porch of the John Marion and Elizabeth Abercrombie house circa 1905 (in their later years).

Back row left to right: Elizabeth's sister's child, name unknown; Mae Ellen Abercrombie; Elizabeth's sister's daughter, name unknown; Mary Abercrombie; Abercrombie daughter, name unknown; Cam Franklin, spouse of Ellen; Abercrombie daughter, name unknown. Middle row left to right: Rosco Means, one of Elizabeth's sister's children; John Marion Abercrombie; John Willie Abercrombie; Elizabeth Abercrombie; Mary's spouse, name unknown; Ellen Abercrombie Franklin. Front row: All of the six children in the front row are Ellen and Cam Franklin's children.

Joseph Fowler, 1927 (Rick's great-grandfather on his mother's side).

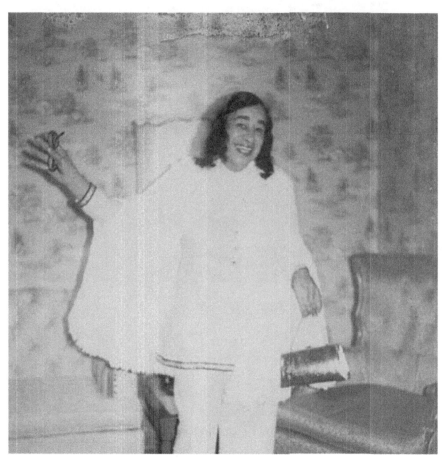

Della Mae Strange (Biggie) circa 1970.
Rick's grandmother on his mother's side.

Eulalia Barrow Bobo (Ruth Moffett with glasses in the background) circa 1970.

Bahá'ís in front of the Benson/Faily home in Greenville circa 1968.
Going clockwise from the top: Charles Abercrombie Sr., Rick Abercrombie, John
Faily, Junie Faily in the pearls, Florence Bagley holding a purse, Stan Bagley seated,
Farzaneh (Fafa) Guillibeaux in front, Jack Guillibeaux in striped sweater, Rachel
Barrick in plaid dress, Fereydoun Jalali on far left, Margaret Quance, Quent Fagans.

The Benson family circa 1972.
Front, left to right: Mark, David, Lang.
Back, left to right: Marzieh, Joy, Dick (Richard)

Youth participants at a Southeast Bahá'í Summer School at Penn Center, circa 1962. Fereydoun took this picture with a timer, and his frustrated expression was due to his exclaiming, "Oh! I forgot to adjust the distance!"

Bottom row from the left: Eileen Lourie, Terri Earl, Phillip Abercrombie, Sam Brody, Betty Lamb, Allen Ward, Steve Milden, Fereydoun Jalali. Second row (1 girl, unknown). Third row from the left: unknown, Joyce Wise, unknown, Jay Voltz, Sandra Knuckles, Carolyn Wells, Gwen Lourie, Madelaine James, unknown, Barbara Green. Top row from the left: Ricky Abercrombie, Anita James, (?) Eilers, Laurie Cohen, Mickey Lamb, (?) Eilers.

Southeastern Bahá'í Summer School at Penn Community Center, 1962
Left to right: Fereydoun Jalali, Ricky Abercrombie; Sam Brodie;
Harry Johnson; . . . Eilers.

Laurie (CJ) Cohen and Phillip Abercrombie. Penn Center Bahá'í SE regional school circa 1965.

Rick and Sara Abercrombie, Penn Center,
Southeastern Regional Winter Bahá'í School, 1965.

A group from one of the many Bahá'í Conferences that my father and I attended. This was probably taken in Greensboro, North Carolina in the mid to late 1960s.

Front row left to right: William (Bill) Tucker; Jack McCants; Adrienne Gordon; Fereydoun Jalali; unknown; Jimmy Robinson; unknown. Second row: Jane Faily; Nancy Searcy (nee Ford); Anna Good; Farzaneh Gillebeaux (nee Rabani); Cammie Thomas; unknown; Helen Thomas. Third row: Daryll Watson; Louise Sawyer; Diane McLaughlin; Coretha Lovell; Grace van der Heidt. Fourth row: Chuck George; William McLaughlin; Yvonne Harrop; Gail Black; unknown; Ava Gordon; Ruth Ballard. Fifth row: Rob (Bob) Berryhill; Herman Freeman; Bernice ("Bunny") Tucker; Margaret Quance; Jean Scales nee Norris; Unknown; Ludmila Van Sombeek; Carlotta Holmes; Jean Brody; Charles Bullock. Top row: unknown; Evander ("Van") Gilmer Jr.

Participants of SE regional Bahá'í School, summer of 1967, Camp Dorothy Walls, NC
Ricky and Sara are on the back row toward the left.

A group from the meeting with the National Spiritual Assembly in the fall of 1969 standing in front of the Bahá'í House of Worship in Wilmette, Illinois. From left to right: Ernestine Mehtzun (nee White), Gwen Clayborne, Firuz Kazemzadeh, Richard Thomas, Bruce Settles, unknown, unknown, Robert Henderson, William (Smitty) Smith, Steve Moore, John (Bo Jack) Mangum, Glenford Mitchell.

About the Authors

As a teenager, **Richard Abercrombie** was the worrisome "bad boy" of a large and conservative African-American family. As he describes, "I was headed to jail or to an early grave" when, to his and everyone's surprise, he experienced a transformation that not only saved his life but also radically changed and enriched the lives of all of his family members. As an adult, he has traveled in Africa, Asia, Europe, and the Middle East in the pursuit of knowledge as well as in service to the Bahá'í Faith, and he has served in a number of elected and appointed positions in the Bahá'í community. Richard currently resides in South Carolina, where he serves on the Local Spiritual Assembly of the Bahá'ís of Greenville and delights everyone with his down-home humor.

JoAnn Borovicka is a freelance researcher, writer, and educational consultant whose creative ventures have included immersion in a wide range of subjects as well as performing and visual art forms. She is the author of *Light of the Kingdom—Biblical Topics in the Bahá'í Writings* and additional interfaith works, a presenter at theology colloquiums and other venues, and a prolific mixed-media artist. JoAnn has served in a number of elected and appointed positions in service to the Bahá'í Faith. When not globe-hopping to visit their world-citizen children, she and her husband, Mike, live in Greenville, South Carolina, where they enjoy the antics of their Miniature Schnauzer, Juniper.